"Dr. Karyn Gordon has written a must-read book for anyone wanting to develop great leadership skills. The book's content is useful as a development tool, to support a team and to help build core skills of great leaders. *The Three Chairs* hooked me from the start with its engaging storytelling, scientific research and abundant actionable tools."

Erin Lukie, Senior Global Director
Young Presidents' Organization (YPO)

"Dr. Karyn is an incredible force for good when it comes to leadership, communication, and building high performance teams. *The Three Chairs: How Great Leaders Drive Communication, Performance and Engagement* is a must read for leaders seeking to implement and an integrated, authentic and effective management process in their organizations, for their high performance teams, and in their personal lives in a changing world."

Scott O'Neil, CEO
Philadelphia 76ers and Author of *Be Where Your Feet Are*

"Dr. Karyn's concept of *The Three Chairs* is brilliant in its simplicity. The way she applies it to leadership skills everywhere, from the classroom to the boardroom, shows her strong grasp of how leaders are not born—they are made."

Michael Gelman, Executive Producer
LIVE with Kelly and Ryan

"This most important, exceptional book will clarify your path forward to becoming a better leader. Dr. Karyn Gordon is THE expert you want to be working with and learning from as you grow your capability. It's a must-read to accelerate your success as a communicator, increase your productivity, and drive engagement."

Courtney Lynch, Co-Founder of Lead Star and
New York Times* Bestselling Author of *Spark:
How to Lead Yourself and Others to Success

"Dr. Karyn's insights on leadership are fresh, timely, and critical for everyone trying to become better leaders. Her *Three Chairs* framework is helpful context for anyone trying to communicate to colleagues and teammates, and also for understanding yourself. I'll definitely be referencing this book and the lessons found within during my one-on-ones!"

Andy Yang, CEO
Indiegogo

"Inspiring yet extremely practical—Dr. Karyn's *The Three Chairs* is a must-read for all entrepreneurs, business leaders, and managers who want practical leadership tools to improve communication and performance with confidence. She has spoken at several EO conferences, and what our members greatly appreciate is how her techniques can apply both to their business and their family."

Don Williams, US Central Region Area Director
EO (Entrepreneurs' Organization) and
CEO of Don Williams Global

"High-performance teams and organizations know that success isn't achieved by accident. Success requires intention and commitment from top to bottom in the organization, and to set that tone in the culture is the job of leadership. Dr. Karyn understands this perfectly, and articulates the lessons successful leaders know and how they apply them in their families and organizations. Any reader looking to improve as a leader will find Dr. Karyn's book both fascinating and helpful."

David Hopkinson, President Team Business Operations
MSG Sports

"In a world with so much information, leaders crave applicable concepts and practical tools to inspire and create great leaders in their organization. Dr. Karyn's *The Three Chairs* is the toolkit! This book will teach you the five core skills great leaders possess. A must-read!"

Molly Fletcher
Former Sports Agent, Author and Speaker

"Family businesses are a specialty, and Dr. Karyn's *The Three Chairs* is the ideal resource. Her knowledge of family systems and organizational systems gives her a unique specialty in this arena—and her latest book is a must-read for all family businesses who want to develop great leaders both in their businesses and in their families."

Janice A. Ruddock, Executive Director
Centre for Family Business

"Whether for a reader or a live audience, Dr. Karyn Gordon provides a fascinating and practical guide on what it takes to become an effective leader. This book is ideal for everyone: from CEOs to interns, parents to students. One can't help but wonder, 'On which chair do I sit'?"

Farah Perelmuter, CEO and Co-Founder
Speakers' Spotlight

"Great leaders are great learners—it's a lifelong journey. If you want to develop leadership for yourself and your teams, Dr. Karyn's *Three Chairs: How Great Leaders Drive Communication, Performance and Engagement* is your go-to resource. I've known Karyn for 20 years, and her gift is being able to teach complex leadership and emotional intelligence research in a practical way to all levels of leaders within organizations, family businesses, and families. *The Three Chairs* is packed with inspiring stories and practical action steps for all of us to become a great leader."

Michael McCain, CEO
Maple Leaf Foods

"Dr. Karyn Gordan is a fantastic coach who has an understanding and empathetic approach. It's great to see her bring these skills to organizational leadership. Anyone who reads this book will find her insightful guidance timely and invaluable."

Desiree Dancy, Chief Diversity Officer and VP
GLG

"In every leadership moment, I must choose which chair I lead from, and that makes all the difference in and for my world. Dr. Karyn has made it easy for us to figure out how to reposition oneself for positive leadership impact. An inspiring and practical read."

John McAuley, CEO
Muskoka Woods and Author of *Leading from the In-Between: Crossing Bridges with Emerging Leaders*

"Recognizing and developing healthy leadership behaviors is a lifelong journey, but *The Three Chairs* accelerates your learning and boosts your self-awareness to make that journey a more fruitful and enjoyable one. Having met Dr. Karyn about five years ago, and first learning about *The Three Chairs,* I have been fortunate to apply what I learned from her both at home and at work. For example, inside our company, we have applied the book's principles to help us further develop a truly team-based culture, with our key leaders occupying the "middle chair" of confidence and equality, and developing future leaders and high-functioning, cross-functional teams across the organization, without silos. Whether your key challenges are more personal, family, or organization-focused, Dr. Karyn's book equips you with the concrete tools you need to figure out who—including yourself—is sitting in which chair, and then take the practical steps necessary to achieve greater success and fulfillment for you, your family, or your team."

Paul Goddard, CEO
Pizza Pizza Limited

"Dr. Karyn's perspective on organizational performance is summed up brilliantly with her '3 chairs' concept. All of us sit in one of these chairs, and any leader seeking to understand their team's strengths and weaknesses and improve results should get to know this. A remarkably easy way to understand the art of communication and a great read for leaders and communicators in any organization!"

Fred Cochran, President
Insula Companies

"As health professionals, our education focuses intently on the technical skill of our profession, but lacks education and preparation for managing people, including employees. Without this skill, business productivity, staff retention, and practice growth can be affected. Dr. Karyn's informative book teaches leadership skills for all types of businesses. My team learned many useful strategies to be better leaders, motivate themselves and others, be more engaged, and deal with conflict resolution in a positive, constructive way."

Dr. Shonna Masse, Pediatric Dentist and Founder
The Children's Dental Centre

"Understanding the concept of Dr. Karyn's *Three Chairs* is an absolute game-changer! It's simple, insightful, and encourages you to look within and take progressive steps to improve your own leadership skills. I'm so excited to promote this in our organization and develop a more efficient and confident management team. *Chi-miigwech* for the continued motivation to make effective change."

Kerri L. King, Human Resource Manager
Mississaugas of the Credit First Nation

"The definition of *leadership* is changing and is now widely used not only in reference to our work lives, but also our private lives. Dr. Karyn's novel depiction of the different styles of leadership based on *The Three Chairs* is simple, yet brilliant in its ease of applicability to all aspects of life. Within the first few pages, you will be able to place yourself on one of those chairs for each of your life's different roles. With this understanding, and with the help of Dr. Karyn's thorough explanations, you can take your first steps in repositioning yourself onto the appropriate chair, at the appropriate times. Dr. Karyn's extensive breadth of knowledge in this area shines through in this book by way of clear and thorough references to the current literature, real-life examples from her work and practice, and, of course, wise words that can only come from mastery of a subject. Bravo, Dr. Karyn!"

Setareh Ziai MD, FRCSC, Co-Founder and Past-President
Canadian Women in Medicine
Assistant Professor of Ophthalmology,
University of Ottawa Eye Institute

"Dr. Karyn's expertise and teachings have improved my business and my marriage, and have provided how-to advice for parenting teenagers to 20-year-olds. Her knowledge of EQ has changed how we provide feedback, handle hard conversations, and help our team deal with anxiety. This book is for anyone that wants to improve all aspects of their life. PERIOD."

William Sturm
President and CEO of Capps, LLC.

"Dr. Karyn is a force of human nature. She is empathetic and intelligent, yet surprisingly simplistic in how she provides you with the tools to better yourself. After reading this book, you will never look at chairs or life the same way."

Tony Chapman
Host of the Podcast *Chatter that Matters*

"Leadership is a lifelong journey of learning and there is no one more committed to equipping leaders with knowledge and know-how than Dr. Karyn. Her book synthesizes the most important and relevant lessons for leaders based on decades of real life experience and research. It's a must-read for any leader who is ready to become exceptional by first nurturing the leader inside each of us."

Caroline Riseboro, President and CEO
Trillium Health Partners Foundation

"Dr. Karyn inspires with a powerful, inclusive reminder that great leadership is learned and equally accessible. A practical toolkit for strengthening communication, attitude and goal-setting, relationships, decision-making, and reducing stress. Dare to pull up your chair and become a better leader!"

Jenn Carkner, Marketing Director
Kellogg's Europe

"Dr. Karyn has a unique gift for explaining leadership principles in a straightforward manner. She also has this amazing ability to connect with folks from all walks of life—from leaders in their field to young people exiting homelessness. Her passion for fostering leadership skills is inspiring."

Dr. Naomi Thulien, Lead Researcher and
***The Identity Project* Scientist**
MAP Centre For Urban Health Solutions

"I've known Dr. Karyn for over 20 years and continue to be impressed at her agility and empathy. She's helped me in corporate settings and with my family. It's great to see her principles being applied in the workplace!"

Richard Burjaw, President
Nestle Professional Canada

THE THREE CHAIRS

CHAIRS

How Great Leaders Drive Communication, Performance, and Engagement

DR. KARYN GORDON

THE THREE CHAIRS:
How Great Leaders Drive Communication,
Performance, and Engagement
by Dr. Karyn Gordon
1. BUS030000 2. BUS071000 3. BUS041000
ISBN (paperback): 978-1-949642-69-8
ISBN (hardback): 978-1-949642-70-4
EBOOK: 978-1-949642-71-1

Cover design by LEWIS AGRELL

Printed in the United States of America

Authority Publishing
11230 Gold Express Dr. #310-413
Gold River, CA 95670
800-877-1097
www.AuthorityPublishing.com

TABLE OF CONTENTS

PART III
THE IMPACT OF GREAT LEADERSHIP ON AN ORGANIZATION

ACKNOWLEDGMENTS

To my mom and dad, whose unconditional love and "middle chair" parenting style inspired me in my leadership journey as a child. Thank you—this book would not exist without you.

To my incredible husband of 20 years—Brent, I adore you! Your loyalty, kindness and patience as I wrote this book was unwavering. Thank you for being my rock and continually encouraging me towards my goals.

To my amazing boys—Baron and Chase—I love being your Mom! Thank you for your words of encouragement (*"Mom, are you done yet? Keep going, Mom!"*) as I pushed toward the finish line.

A big thank you to my incredible team of editors, researchers and coordinators who helped me pull all the details together—Marcia, Janelle, Stephanie, Chela, and Tifani—you each have strengths I do not have and I'm deeply grateful for all of you.

A deep thank you to all our organizational and family clients who have trusted me to coach them in their leadership journey over the last two decades. Doing this kind of work is such a joy and is truly my life's purpose.

And finally—a huge thank you to Robert Herjavec for writing the foreword and sharing your own personal leadership journey with *The Three Chairs*. Your story is truly inspiring—and a beautiful example—that great leadership is a process of learning and growing towards the middle chair, and that it's possible for all of us!

FOREWORD BY ROBERT HERJAVEC

Successful leaders are made, not born—I'm sure of it. The difference between successful leaders and unsuccessful leaders is the mindset to learn, apply, and go. It's training and enthusiasm. If you have enough energy and desire, and follow great guidance, you will amaze yourself. I talk about successful leaders in my books *You Don't Have to Be a Shark: Creating Your Own Success, The Will To Win: Leading, Competing, Succeeding,* and *Driven: How to Succeed In Business and Life,* but here is my own leadership journey as it relates to *The Three Chairs.*

Anyone who has heard my story knows that I was born in Yugoslavia, now Croatia, and emigrated to Canada with my parents when I was eight. My father was an outspoken anti-Communist who had been jailed 22 times and it got to a point where it was no longer safe for us to live there. So we left the farm I had known all my life, and my grandmother who was helping to raise me, and moved into a family friend's basement apartment outside of Toronto.

None of us knew English, and we were suddenly thrown into a new environment, a new way of life, and we had to adapt. My father walked to work every day to earn $76 a week at a factory job. He was a really tough guy who didn't complain and who wouldn't allow me to complain either. He taught me to be grateful and that all people deserve an opportunity—so work hard and persevere.

That experience was transformative for me, because I decided at an early age that I did not want to be poor. It wasn't so much that I wanted to be rich, but I definitely did not want to struggle financially the way I saw my parents struggle.

Looking back, I suspect those early life experiences, and my parents' guidance, helped me find a seat in the middle chair. Dr. Karyn's description of a middle chair mindset—wanting to have a better life, being willing to work for it, not seeing myself as a victim—resonated with me. Although I didn't know at the time that I was positioning myself for success, I did start to see that I was on the right path.

An advantage I had was that I had mentors. I've actually had many mentors throughout my career but the most important was my first mentor, my father. He taught me the importance of working hard, sacrificing, and surrounding yourself with people who inspire you to do your best work. He showed me what it meant to be courageous—to leave everything you've ever known for the possibility of a better life for your family, your child. And he showed me that I could make it happen.

So, after graduating from the University of Toronto, I held a number of minimum wage jobs to pay the bills and support my own family. I did some freelance work on a few TV shows but needed to find an income source in between productions, so I applied for a job at Logiquest selling IBM computer equipment. I wasn't qualified, but I knew I could do it, so I offered to work for free for six months to prove myself. At night I waited tables to earn money to live. Logiquest was where I learned the computer industry, and I was good at it. I was promoted several times until I became general manager.

I left Logiquest in 1990 and started my own company, BRAK Systems, which was an integrator of internet security software. Although I started it as a home-based business, we grew rapidly. Ten years later, AT&T Canada bought the business for $30.2 million.

Not sure I wanted to start a new company right away, I joined Ramp Network as vice president of sales, until it was sold to Nokia soon after and I was again out of job.

Clear that I should control my own destiny, I founded The Herjavec Group, which is now Canada's largest information security company.

My success as an entrepreneur is what caught the eye of producers for the Canadian business show "Dragon's Den," where I participated as an investor in seasons one through six, and which is very similar to the US show "Shark Tank," which I later joined.

Although it's a TV program, the person you see on screen is the man I am in real life. I try to be fair in my offers, kind in my feedback, and encouraging to all entrepreneurs who come on the show to secure an investment. I'm clear about the type of people I want to work with—both entrepreneurs and fellow investors. I'd say that at least half the time an entrepreneur steps on the set, I make up my mind in the first couple of minutes whether I'm interested in partnering with them. I look for confidence and poise. I want to invest in someone who is self-assured, not arrogant.

A confident leader is authentic in terms of who they are, what their values are, and clear about their goals. They are resilient. They are self-disciplined, passionate, humble, curious, solve problems, ask questions, take risks, persevere in failure, and deal with their fears. They listen, create value for people, serve others, and aim for greatness. They understand the world does not reward mediocrity, so they work towards creating exceptional results. Essentially, I'm looking for people who sit in the middle chair, and who have a great business, because that's where great leaders sit and where I try to sit as well.

That's not to say I've always sat in the middle chair—I haven't. There have been times in my life when I've felt unworthy, like a failure, depressed, and didn't know how to move on from those feelings. I used to think if you were compassionate, you were weak. But when I reached out to my friend for advice in how to move on, he told me, "To help yourself, you need to serve other people."

He was right. Volunteering at a Seattle homeless shelter taught me gratitude and compassion and empathy. I had noise in my life and I couldn't see straight. Connecting with others, serving them, reminded me of who I really was. It gave me back purpose. Focusing on helping others turned my life around, and helped me move back into the middle chair.

One of our greatest battles for becoming a successful leader is ourselves—because we self-sabotage. We are full of doubt and fear. Yet the more we can stay focused on being the best version of ourselves, and serving others with our skills and resources, the more time we will spend in that middle chair—the chair of leaders.

As you'll learn in *The Three Chairs*, we all sit in different chairs during the different seasons of our lives. To be a successful leader in the middle chair, you have to find clarity about who you are, what makes you tick, who you want to become, what skills you want to learn, and be a real student of success to get ahead. You have to learn to communicate with others, be confident, listen, never give up, stay focused, and always learn.

Anyone can become a successful leader. There is nothing special about me. You just have to have the desire to go out there. We are each our own greatest asset, capable of becoming great leaders. My favorite word is "Go," and I hope you go and learn to become a great leader who sits in the middle chair.

PREFACE

MY WHY

"There are only two ways to influence human behavior:
you can manipulate it or you can inspire it."

—Simon Sinek, speaker and author of *Start with Why*

My purpose is developing great leaders—both in organizations and families. I'm passionate about this because great leadership is learned, which gives us all tremendous hope that we can better ourselves, and because it impacts every part of our lives. Leadership involves many skills—technical as well as emotional, including emotional intelligence and people skills. Leadership capabilities can be developed, and they can determine your success in your career and at home. According to the *Harvard Business Review*[1], "Studies have shown that a high emotional quotient (EQ) boosts career success, entrepreneurial potential, leadership talent, health, relationships, satisfaction, humor, and happiness." EQ is the secret sauce for great leaders.

Great leadership is a journey that starts in childhood and requires a lifelong process of learning new skills. My personal journey is an example of how children can begin to learn some of these foundational leadership abilities. Although I now speak and coach executives on great leadership, many are surprised to know that I struggled in school as a child. In fact, I shared my story as part of a keynote I once gave at a conference, and Scott O'Neil, CEO of the Philadelphia 76ers NBA basketball team, was so enamored with it that he asked to include it in his book, *Be Where Your Feet Are: Seven Principles to Keep You Present, Grounded and Thriving*.

My own leadership story begins in the eighth grade, when, after working extremely hard in school, the grades I received were much lower than I had hoped or expected. My parents knew I had been applying myself, so they decided to have me tested by an educational consultant. I'll never forget the day that I met with him, hoping to learn why I was having so much trouble in my classes.

"Well, Karyn, I know what the problem is. You have a learning disability and, to be honest, I think you will be lucky to finish high school." I was utterly devastated by his message and unempathetic tone. At 13, I felt my heart sink as I pictured all of my goals and dreams disappearing. Fortunately, my parents knew exactly how to inspire and lead me.

After faith, education was my family's highest value. My father earned his doctorate from Princeton; my mother went back to school in her fifties to earn a master's in counseling; and my grandmother had become a medical doctor in the 1940s— frequently the only woman in many of her classes. My older sister and brother are both gifted and thrived in school. Education was also something I valued highly—and I felt like I was letting myself down.

But my parents processed this experience very differently. They saw the consultant's report as "data"—rather than defining who I was, it was simply feedback about how I learn. They also understood the importance of focusing on effort, not outcomes. They told me, "Karyn, starting today, we will never ask to see your report card. You cannot control your grades, but you can control your effort, 100 percent. So, instead, when it's report card day we will have one simple question for you: 'Did you do your absolute best?' You *can* control that, so we will hold you accountable to that standard." This approach would not work for every child, but it worked for me.

In that moment, my parents' words instilled hope. They were right. I could control my effort and my time management—setting realistic goals, taking initiative, asking for help, and understanding my learning disability. My mindset shifted. I focused on my own progress, dropped my previous resistance to requesting help from teachers, and, with new tools, saw steady improvement. That progress fueled my motivation, translating into ever-rising grades. Despite the consultant's prognosis, I not only finished high school, I graduated from university and subsequently earned my doctorate. The key was my parents' philosophy: Holding people accountable for what they can control empowers them, emboldens them, and inspires them to do their best. This is one of the foundations of great leadership.

At 13, I saw my disability as a curse; today I see it as a blessing because it taught me some of the leadership EQ skills I will be teaching you in this book. You'll hear about the importance of setting realistic goals, taking initiative, seeking input, studying poor feedback as "data," asking for help, and surrounding yourself with others who can support you in achieving your goals.

One benefit of my disability is that it taught me how to simplify and teach information in a clear way that reaches more people, such as by using visual imagery, charts, acronyms, metaphors, and stories. I always start with research and then focus on how to apply it in practice, so that people can develop and grow.

I share my why here so that you know we can all learn great leadership EQ skills if we have the hunger to grow—regardless of your age, title, education, race, gender, or any other characteristic. It doesn't matter whether you are an emerging leader in your twenties or a boomer CEO of your organization—the goal of *The Three Chairs* is to both inspire and equip you with practical tools to develop great leadership in yourself and those around you.

INTRODUCTION

WHAT YOU WILL LEARN

"Self-awareness and self-love matter.
Who we are is how we lead."

—Brené Brown, research professor and author of *Dare to Lead: Brave Work. Tough Conversations. Whole Hearts.*

In this book you'll learn that leadership starts with self-awareness. You need to know yourself before you can effectively lead others. You'll learn what The Three Chairs are and how they relate to being a great leader. You'll learn how The Three Chairs impact nearly every part of your life and determine the kind of leader you are, through your communication, productivity, risk-taking, and relationships.

The science behind the concept is based on enormous amounts of research, to the point that you can make educated guesses on how you think people will respond to situations based on which chair they sit in. You'll learn how to build the five core skills of great leaders in yourself and in your team. You'll learn the impact of great leadership on an organization.

Although this book is focused on helping you determine which chair you're currently sitting in and then supporting you in developing as a leader, it will also help you improve your team's communication, productivity, and engagement. Reading it together as a group can help develop a common language with which to discuss leadership and decision-making. To assist you in applying all that you'll learn in the book, there is a free downloadable workbook and many other bonus resources (videos, Q&A, discussion questions) for you and your team. You'll find them at www.dkleadership.org/thethreechairs.

This is a business leadership book, but the principles you'll learn are transferable to your personal life, helping to improve your relationships with your partner, your children, your family, and your friends. Being a great leader can improve every aspect of your life.

PART I

WHAT IS A GREAT LEADER?

Great leadership is simply a set of skills that are first learned internally, which means all of us can develop it. Great leadership is not about having a title. In fact, a title or supervisory role is simply an external opportunity for a person to exercise and strengthen their leadership skills. A job is not going to suddenly bestow leadership abilities on you—you have to acquire those on your own.

Becoming a great leader starts in childhood. From there it is a process of recognizing skill gaps, blind spots, finding the tools and resources to close the skill gaps, and continually working toward becoming a great leader.

Great leaders invest time and energy working on themselves. They identify the skills they need to be better leaders and they pursue the opportunity to learn how to manage themselves and others more effectively.

You already have the power within you to become a great leader; you may just need specific tools to be added or sharpened in your "Great Leadership Toolbox." Great leadership is a lifelong journey.

1

UNDERSTANDING THE
THREE CHAIRS

"Changing an organization, a company, a country—or a world—begins with the simple step of changing yourself."

—Tony Robbins, author of *Awaken the Giant Within: How to Take Immediate Control of Your Mental, Emotional, Physical and Financial Destiny!*

W e all have the capacity, the potential, to be great leaders, though we have to learn to develop it, to one degree or another. Most people assume you have to rise through the ranks or be given a lofty title in order to be a superior leader. They're wrong. Anyone can be a leader, no matter their title, current role, industry, background, ethnicity, gender, or age. But to be a *great* leader takes a lot of work. It also takes self-reflection, a desire to learn, and the skills and discipline to know what to do. Becoming a great leader is an ongoing process, not a destination. It's also a challenge, especially since research from the *Journal of Behavioral Science*[2] shows that 70 percent of adults suffer from imposter syndrome—of feeling inadequate and believing they're not worthy of their current position or circumstance.

THE SELF-CONFIDENCE AND DECISION-MAKING LINK

I've been coaching CEOs, senior executives, emerging leaders, new managers, and high-performance professionals and teams for more than 20 years, in nearly every industry, with a specialty in family business. Most business leaders come to me for leadership development—specifically to improve performance, learn effective communication, manage the multi-generational workforce, and equip new managers to drive engagement and retention. My purpose and my passion is developing great leaders.

But my work with great leaders actually began when I was a counselor helping teenagers, who are now millennials. I launched my coaching practice at age 22 after finishing an undergrad in psychology and a master's in counseling; I later completed my doctorate in marriage and family. My practice was in a medical building working alongside three family physicians and, because of my proximity to private healthcare practices, I quickly attracted referrals from doctors in the building.

Over time, more than 100 physicians were sending me clients. Most of those clients were teenagers grappling with anxiety, lack of confidence, depression, and relationship issues. And because I was solutions-oriented—teaching specific skills that got results—in no time, my practice was full and I'd earned a reputation as a successful changemaker.

One day in particular, however, I felt like I was in the movie "Groundhog Day," because in every single meeting, my teen clients said nearly the same exact thing: they had a toxic mindset, felt they could never please anyone, and were extremely stressed from trying to be perfect. They all had such unhealthy thought patterns.

Something had to be done. This was a widespread problem that wasn't getting any better.

I started by researching how attitude impacts decision-making and tracked down dozens of different research studies. Imposter syndrome was a big piece of the puzzle, it turned out.

Because many people don't see themselves as capable, they may not set gutsy goals, ask for raises, take job promotions, or make decisions that are not in their best interest. For example, did you know that confidence impacts how much people earn? Research from the *Journal of Vocational Behavior*[3] found that the more confident people are in their occupational tasks, the higher the salary they can earn three and seven years into their careers. An unhealthy mindset affects everything.

Ultimately, after poring over the research, I identified three main attitudes that drive how we behave. These attitudes affect goal-setting, risk-taking, relationships, communication, time management, self-discipline, and self-care, among

> ATTITUDES IMPACT FEELINGS, WHICH IMPACT PERFORMANCE.

other things. I call these three attitudes the blind, the disguised, and the confident, and I picture them each sitting in different chairs.

Origins of The Three Chairs

In thinking about how best to present these new concepts to teens, I decided to set up a short skit using a talk show format, which I performed on auditorium stages in high schools. I positioned three chairs facing the audience, for three volunteers to sit in—one in the left chair, one on the right, and one in the middle.

4

I then asked for volunteers from the audience to act out the roles in my abbreviated one-act play. Later, when I taught business leaders this concept, I would simply place three chairs on the stage without actors, like the cover of this book. I learned most adults don't like improvisational acting, but greatly appreciated the visual of The Three Chairs; I pointed to the chairs when explaining each one's character and attitude, and how those impact leadership.

Blind attitude –
acts inferior to others

In the left chair was the character we'll call Susan. Susan reflects the blind attitude. She feels and acts inferior to others because she is blind to her own uniqueness. She has low self-confidence and constantly puts herself down. She is extremely hard on herself, critical of everything she thinks or does. When people put her down, she believes them and, consequently, doesn't respond or defend herself. She frequently apologizes, blaming herself for anything that goes awry, even if it is beyond her control.

Disguised attitude –
acts superior to others

In the right chair, Mark represents the disguised attitude. He acts superior and arrogant toward others. He is cocky, cutting people off in order to make his point, and puts everyone else down. When speaking to others, he communicates in thought, word, and tone that he is better than they are. In addition to being condescending, Mark is not open to feedback or to other people's ideas. This is the disguised attitude because in public these individuals appear overly confident, but if you take the mask off, most Marks are grappling with enormous insecurity.

Confident attitude –
acts equal to others

In the middle chair is Chris, who has a confident attitude. As a result, he acts like an equal, a peer, around others. Unlike Susan, insults don't impact Chris, because he has a positive mindset. If Mark tried to belittle or bully him, Chris holds his ground and respectfully challenges him. He has a powerful inner strength.

Chris has a solid sense of self and knows that negative talk is a reflection of the other person, not him. He has an attitude of equality, viewing himself as no better or worse than anyone else. He pursues excellence, not perfection, and his self-worth is not based on achievement. He is a positive force who encourages and lifts others, even when they make mistakes. With respect to the others in the two chairs, Chris routinely encourages Susan and, unlike Mark, does not put anyone down. In fact, Chris is one of the few people willing to respectfully stand up to Mark when he makes snarky comments.

After the skit, I explain what each character thinks and feels, how that impacts their decision-making on a daily basis, and, most importantly, how each attendee can represent the middle chair themselves, since this attitude is learned.

I taught my Three Chairs concept for years in elementary, middle, and high schools. About 90 percent of my audiences understood it in less than five minutes—the length of the skit. You could see their eyes light up as they recognized where they sat and guessed where their family and friends were sitting. Then I shifted to teaching it to business leaders and how it impacts leadership. Audiences from kindergarteners to business professionals could immediately identify which chair they typically occupy, once I explained the dynamics. It's so simple and yet so powerful!

THE POWER OF ATTITUDES

The reason attitudes are so powerful is that how we think—our thoughts—impact how we feel—our feelings—which impact our performance and the decisions we make on a daily basis—our actions. Our attitude causes a domino effect in every aspect of our life. So before I explain how these attitudes impact decision-making, take a moment and ask yourself this key question:

Which chair do you sit in the *majority* of the time and how does that impact your life?

HOW THESE ATTITUDES IMPACT LEADERSHIP CAPACITY

Helping audiences understand the three attitudes—blind (left chair), disguised (right chair), and confident (middle chair)—is pretty simple. More challenging is helping audiences not only understand how these attitudes impact performance and leadership capabilities but most important—how to change them. Helping audiences learn how to sit in the middle chair, and how they can help others sit in the middle chair, is the true purpose of this book. Why? Because that's where great leaders sit.

The chair you're seated in affects a laundry list of aspects of your life, but there are five areas that are significantly impacted by your attitude: communication, goal-setting, relationships, decision-making, and stress. Let's take a quick high-level look at all five areas, since you may sit in the middle chair in some parts of your life, and in the left or right chair in other areas. Be your own evaluator. Also, it is important to know that The Three Chairs are not like three boxes. They are more fluid—like a continuum or spectrum.

Communication

In thinking about how communication is affected by the chair you're sitting in, put yourself in the mindset of someone who is in each chair. How would they react? If you're sitting in the left chair, where you're unsure of yourself, imagine how you'd respond if someone suggests you've made a big mistake.

Let's say that person pointing out your error is Jake. If you're Susan, sitting in the left chair, you're likely going to blame yourself for anything that has gone wrong. You may also go complain to someone else about what Jake has just said to you.

On the other hand, if you're Mark, sitting in the right chair, and acting superior to everyone else in the office, you may tell

Jake, "You are the problem," as you go on the offensive. You likely blame Jake or others in your department—anyone else—for what has occurred, because this couldn't possibly be your fault.

And yet, if you're Chris, sitting in the middle chair, you are more likely to be assertive with Jake. You'll likely ask him a lot of questions. You are colleagues, after all, and you want to understand what's going on so you can help; whose fault it is doesn't matter to you. You're focused on solving the problem, not rehashing who did what.

Not only does this confident, respectful, assertive approach work better to solve problems—it builds the team dynamic. According to *Business and Professional Communication Quarterly*[4], leaders who are assertive and focused on problem-solving receive higher ratings from group members.

Goal-Setting

How you think about yourself also affects how risk-averse you are, which affects your career trajectory. So, if you're Susan and sitting in the left chair, you may not take risks at all, since you don't want the possibility of failure. Conversely, you may set goals that are so high as to be unrealistic. This then feeds your performance anxiety, because you think you're likely to fail with such a high-performance goal. This unrealistic perfectionism mindset often plagues and paralyses you. You may look like you sit in the middle chair but, behind the mask, you feel enormous anxiety trying to achieve external success.

Mark, in the right chair, behaves similarly. Although Mark appears self-assured, deep down he's likely as insecure as Susan—maybe even more so. He avoids taking risks and setting goals that could lead to failure, or sets outrageous goals, not taking into account any possible danger or how his behavior may impact him and those around him. He has little empathy toward others. If he takes a risk and fails, he rarely believes it is his fault.

And then there's Chris. He sets realistic goals for himself—stretching but attainable. He strives for excellence but is humble, even when successful. He sees failure simply as data from which he can learn. As a result, Chris is fearless about setting goals—and is more likely to achieve them. People who are confident have higher goal-setting skills, which is then associated with higher productivity and performance, the *Journal of Applied Psychology*[5] reported.

Relationships

Your confidence also shapes the relationships you form at work, with coworkers, business partners, and even in personal relationships. Insecure people, who are sitting in the left chair, often see their relationships in absolute, all-or-nothing terms, using language such as "always" and "never," reported the *Journal of Personality and Social Psychology*[6], and are less likely to welcome suggestions, according to research published in the *Harvard Business Review*[7].

Arrogant leaders sitting in the right chair also struggle in their relationships. Researchers from the University of Akron and Michigan State University[8] found that arrogant leaders are "associated with low self-esteem" and use their arrogance to mask insecurities. They discount feedback, avoid blame, and "make interpersonal interactions difficult," which creates a stressful culture.

In contrast, great leaders in the middle chair highly value their relationships. They listen, seek to understand, admit their mistakes, and are open to feedback, because they realize that while they know a lot, they don't know everything. They have a powerfully humble mindset and because of it, people want to work with and for them.

Despite these differences between The Three Chairs, interestingly, people are often attracted to those who sit in the same chair as they do, or the one opposite. Why? Because we are often attracted to others who are like-minded and share our views, found researchers at Wellesley College and the University of Kansas[9].

Of course, there are exceptions. However, people in the left chair are often attracted to others in the left or in the right chair. Because those in the left chair often have difficulty standing up for themselves and see themselves as unworthy, those in the right chair often confirm that perception. Similarly, those in the right chair can be controlling and manipulative in their relationships and are often attracted to people in the right or left chair, because those in the left chair are willing to put up with it and are afraid to give feedback, which makes it a match.

People in the middle chair typically prefer to be with other people in the middle chair because they highly value all people equally—themselves and others—and want to be around others who share that view.

Decision-making

Where you're sitting also drives how you use your time—how you prioritize, approach tasks, and get work done. Employees in the left chair, like Susan, who are unsure of themselves, often have a hard time making decisions and setting boundaries. They are less likely to say no to requests from others.

Employees in the right chair, like Mark, are typically the people handing off work to those in the left chair, because they can. They make demands on others as a way to demonstrate their superiority, often acting like dictators.

Employees in the middle chair are often extremely productive because they are capable of distinguishing between critical and less important tasks. They have no problem saying no when it's called for. They are highly disciplined, decisive, aim for excellence rather than perfection in their decisions, empower those around them and take others' feelings into account when making decisions. Employees with higher confidence, known as psychological capital, were judged by their managers to have higher levels of productivity and performance, as reported the *Leadership and Organizational Development Journal*[10].

Stress

The chair you're sitting in also impacts the amount of stress you feel and how you manage it. Employees like Susan, sitting in the left chair, often feel stressed and overwhelmed. They generally have a hard time saying no to requests, put others' needs above their own, internalize the stress, and are tough on themselves.

Employees on the right, like Mark, often push work onto others' shoulders—both to enhance their own productivity and to share responsibility with others if there is any degree of failure. When their stress levels rise, they are more likely to communicate harshly or blame others.

People in the middle chair, however, have often mastered boundary-setting skills, such as saying "no" to requests that are unreasonable or simply not possible given their workload. They prioritize self-care, understanding that taking care of themselves is a requirement for high performance. Their self-confidence is positively linked to lower stress and anxiety, positive emotions, and overall well-being, according to the *Journal of Leadership and Organizational Studies*[11].

WHICH CHAIR ARE YOU SITTING IN THE MAJORITY OF THE TIME?

We are each sitting in one of those three chairs, though we may switch in different environments or the role we're currently playing. It doesn't matter your age, title, gender, ethnicity, education level, or years of experience. Your current chair is based on your attitude.

You might be the CEO of a multimillion-dollar business, sitting in the right chair, and, as a result, people find it difficult to work for you. Your retention and engagement are poor, your family and kids are put off by you, and your relationships are often unsatisfying. Or you could be a senior leader in the left chair but, behind the mask, you struggle with enormous perfectionism, anxiety, and lack of boundaries. Or you could be an emerging leader in your 20s, just getting your career started, and sitting in the middle chair. You could have an incredible mindset, be highly disciplined, assertive, take initiative, be encouraging to others, and be the manager everyone else wants to work with. Age and experience have little bearing on the chair you're sitting in right now.

No one sits in the middle chair 100 percent of the time, since that would be perfection and perfection doesn't exist. A confident person often sits in the middle chair 80 to 90 percent of the time.

The Three Chairs is a self-awareness tool, to help all levels of leaders think about their attitude and how it impacts their leadership and performance. And while it is helpful to reflect on where colleagues, teams, bosses, clients and even family members may sit—I strongly recommend that you ask others for their opinion, rather than telling them where you think they sit.

> THINK OF A GREAT LEADER YOU ADMIRE. WHICH CHAIR ARE THEY SITTING IN? BASED ON THE RESPONSES I'VE RECEIVED FROM THOUSANDS OF PEOPLE, IT IS VERY LIKELY THAT PERSON IS SEATED IN THE MIDDLE CHAIR.

WHAT ARE THE SKILLS NEEDED TO MOVE INTO THE MIDDLE CHAIR?

Behind the concept of The Three Chairs is "emotional intelligence," or EQ, which psychologist, science journalist, and author Daniel Goleman[12] describes as "the ability to...understand your effect on others and manage yourself accordingly, accounts for 90 percent of what moves people up the ladder when IQ and technical skills are roughly similar."

Employees can be brilliant with great technical skills, suggesting a high intelligence quotient (IQ), but have very poor people skills, or emotional intelligence, so people don't want to work with them. If you want to be a great leader who sits in the middle chair, IQ is still important; intelligence does play a role. But emotional intelligence, or EQ, plays an even bigger role.

EQ is simply a set of learned skills. My CARDS™ acronym spells out the five components of emotional intelligence and how they align with The Three Chairs. I consider CARDS™ to be the five leadership EQ skills.

The 5 Leadership EQ Skills™	Left Chair	Middle Chair	Right Chair
	Blind attitude	Confident attitude	Disguised attitude
Communication	More likely to be passive (keep quiet and avoid) or passive-aggressive (talking to others behind their back).	More likely to be assertive, and respectful. More likely to seek to understand, focus on problem-solving, and take responsibility for their part. People want to work with them because they are positive and honest with feedback.	More likely to be aggressive, blaming, and to attack others. More likely to cut people off, not listen or seek to understand.

Attitude and goal-setting	More likely to set few goals or goals that are too high. They often struggle with perfectionism and focus on things they cannot control, such as other people and outcomes.	More likely to set realistic-but-stretch goals. They often focus on excellence, not perfection. More likely to set goals on things they can control, such as their attitude and actions, and achieve them.	More likely to set goals with little empathy for how their decisions impact others. More likely to blame others if goals are not reached.
Relationships	More likely to see relationships in all-or-nothing terms. More likely to be attracted to those who think like them (blind or disguised) in relationships.	More likely to be humble, ask for feedback, open to suggestion and lift others. More likely to inspire others. More likely to be attracted to those who think like them (confident) in relationships.	More likely to act arrogantly in their relationships, discount feedback and blame others. More likely to try to control and manipulate others. More likely to be attracted to those who think like them (blind or disguised) in relationships.
Decision-making	More likely to be indecisive, due to fear of failure, have difficulty saying "no," setting boundaries, and trying to win the approval of others.	More likely to be decisive, based on values and goals, have clear boundaries, and communicate them. More likely to take initiative on realistic-yet-stretch goals.	More likely to set goals that are too high or too low, making unrealistic perfectionist demands of themselves and others.

| Stress | More likely to believe their self-worth is based externally, not internally, which causes a lot of stress. Often has difficulty saying "no" and seeks approval of others. More likely not to prioritize self-care, thus risking burnout. | More likely to be masters of emotion management. More likely to believe their self-worth is based on who they are and not what they achieve. More likely to have confidence to say no, feel calm under pressure, have lower stress, and prioritize self-care. | More likely to believe their self-worth is based externally, not internally, which causes a lot of stress. More likely to lash out at others when they are stressed. |

Chapter 1 Action Steps: Apply the learning! Complete the exercise in *The Three Chairs: Workbook* and *Team Discussion Questions*. Go to www.dkleadership.org/thethreechairs for these bonus tools.

2

WHO CAN BECOME A GREAT LEADER?

"Leadership is not about titles, positions, or flowcharts.
It is about one life influencing another."

—John C. Maxwell, leadership expert and author of *Becoming a Person of Influence: How to Positively Impact the Lives of Others*

Being a great leader starts with managing yourself well, by effectively juggling your many roles and priorities. My client Dwayne could have been the poster child for poor performing leadership and close to burnout, due to his personal habits. But the truth is, Dwayne's name could just as easily have been Jerry or Marcia or Lee. Dwayne's story is like so many other leaders' stories.

This CEO of a fast-growing tech company needed executive coaching, he believed, but he quickly realized that change was needed in nearly every aspect of his life—not just at work. Things were off-balance. His priorities were misaligned. And he was overwhelmed by what he needed to accomplish every day. To be a better leader, a great leader, he needed to make some changes in how he was spending his time. At the outset, there really was no structure to his day. When we started working together, Dwayne was stressed and anxious. He felt that he was not getting much done; his productivity was mediocre at best, despite working around the clock. He knew he could do better, but he didn't know where to begin.

He connected quickly to The Three Chair concept and identified that he was sitting in all three chairs—in different ways. He used to sit more in the middle chair he shared, but when his company grew fast, he had a hard time saying no, setting boundaries, didn't prioritize self-care (left chair) so then quickly felt overwhelmed and became aggressive in his communication to his team and family (right chair). His choices were negatively impacting his performance as a business leader and he was allowing his business to manage him instead of him managing his business. He wanted to get back to the middle chair, where he was in control again and could empower his team in this new growth stage of the business.

So together we started by assessing his values and how he was managing his time. How was he spending his days and nights, and what was he getting done? The problem became fairly obvious as he talked about his daily routine. He was not managing his time according to his values or priorities, and this was adversely impacting his energy level.

Dwayne's typical day started in the morning at the office, where he jumped into back-to-back meetings as soon as he set foot in the door. He was pulled in many different directions simultaneously as he tried to meet his employees' information needs. By the end of the day, Dwayne was worn out but had completed few of his own tasks. So he'd bring them home.

He'd arrive home late, quickly eat dinner, and then open his laptop to work late into the night, playing catch-up on all the issues that had cropped up while he was in meetings, all but ignoring his wife and kids in the process. Because Dwayne continued to work into the evening, he ended up sending out emails late at night. Consequently, his employees felt that they too were expected to work 24/7. When they did get some of Dwayne's time face-to-face, he frequently snapped at them or was overly critical. As a result, they slowly stopped interacting with him. Morale at the company was on the decline and the culture was becoming unhealthy and toxic. Dwayne recognized what was going on but didn't know how to turn things around.

CREATING CLEAR VALUES AND AN EFFECTIVE ROUTINE

At the root of all of Dwayne's challenges was a lack of clear values, coupled with poor self-management. His values were family, health, and growth—yet his values were not aligned with his time; when that happens, research shows it will impact your life satisfaction, happiness, and performance. By restructuring his day to reflect his values, he saw results almost immediately.

RESEARCH FROM THE *JOURNAL OF PERSONALITY*[13] FOUND THAT LIFE SATISFACTION AND POSITIVITY INCREASED WHEN PEOPLE LIVE ACCORDING TO THEIR VALUES AND THEIR DEFINITION OF SUCCESS. IN ADDITION, RESEARCH CITED IN *HARVARD BUSINESS REVIEW*[4] REPORTED THAT WHEN PEOPLE HAVE A POSITIVE MINDSET, PERFORMANCE IMPROVES THROUGH INCREASED PRODUCTIVITY, ENGAGEMENT, AND CREATIVITY.

Dwayne's goal was to create a routine that leveraged when he had the most energy and aligned with his values of family, health, and growth, which included higher productivity and reduced stress. He needed to shift from being led by everyone else's priorities to managing his own priorities.

In this redesign, the first step was looking at when he was most effective. That was early morning, he said, so he blocked off that time for high-level thinking. Instead of rushing to the office to attend other people's meetings, Dwayne created a new morning routine for himself. After a 15-minute meditation first thing in the morning to prepare for the day, Dwayne had breakfast and then worked from 6:00 am to 9:00 am from his newly-outfitted home office. He turned his cell phone off and dedicated himself to completing the type of big picture strategizing that he, as CEO, needed to do. At 9:00 am, he headed to the office and began working with his team, so that they could be more productive. Growth topped Dwayne's values, which could be achieved by helping his team improve its performance as a whole.

Around 5:00 pm, Dwayne headed out to do some yoga. In addition to helping him better manage his stress, yoga was also a transitional activity that helped him shift his thinking away from work to his family. It also reflected the high value he placed on his health; until then, he had been ignoring his health. He and his family began having dinner together around 6:30. During this time, he kept his laptop shut and cell phone off. His focus was on his family and nothing else. His evening was his refueling time—meaning no more evening work. He needed this time to reenergize so that he could be ready for his early morning work routine. It was surprising how quickly their whole family dynamic changed for the better with this new process.

Interestingly, Dwayne had initially been resistant and skeptical. But he agreed to try it for three days. Typically, when clients agree to commit to a new habit for three consecutive days, during which they start to experience the benefits, it gives them the traction they need to continue it. After three days, Dwayne was hooked. He felt more energized, focused, productive, and calm. He was clear about what he wanted and was making decisions according to his values. This simple plan was a "game-changer" for him. He was moving toward sitting in the middle chair.

THE RIPPLE EFFECT

Within a few weeks, Dwayne's senior management team wanted to hear about his new approach to work. Having seen how productive he had suddenly become, they wanted to know his secret. He was available, engaged, less stressed, and more encouraging as a boss. Whatever he was doing, it was working and they wanted in. As they adopted his approach, the whole company culture began to shift. There was a ripple effect.

Because Dwayne stopped emailing employees late at night, they, too, could reclaim that time for themselves—for relaxation and rejuvenation. Their productivity began to climb as their stress levels dropped. The company's overall performance also improved, which lifted everyone's attitude, inspiring additional positive changes.

So what had been the spark? Dwayne's new routine and reduced stress energized him. When he arrived at work, he was able to focus on the needs of his team, since his work had been taken care of earlier that morning. He could help everyone make decisions and make progress on their tasks, which propelled the whole company forward. In a nutshell, he could lead.

Now, he was optimistic, thoughtful in his responses, and able to give everyone his full attention when he was in the office. After digging out from his feelings of overwhelm and poor work habits, Dwayne could finally be a great leader. He could serve his employees and give them the support they wanted and needed. And he could be a role model for effective self-management techniques that others in his employ could also adopt.

Turns out, it matters when things are done. Daniel Pink confirms this in his book *When*, through his research into biological and circadian rhythms. Pink discovered that important decisions should never be made in the afternoon, when our collective mood is gloomier. Mornings, he discovered, are best for brain work, in part because it is a time of day when we are optimistic and feeling good. Afternoons, when we are generally at our worst, are better for more mundane tasks. Dwayne had arranged his schedule so that he could function at his highest level.

THE IMPORTANCE OF SELF-CARE

By taking better care of himself, Dwayne was able to be a great leader to those around him. Self-care is essential for all great leaders. Remember the emergency instructions that flight attendants give before the airplane you're on takes off? "In the case of an emergency, put your own oxygen mask on first." That's not being selfish, it's making it possible for you to remain conscious so that you can help everyone else around you.

The same is true of great leaders. Before you can be available mentally and emotionally to support your team, you need to be mentally, emotionally, and physically equipped yourself.

Gallup's recent book, *It's the Manager*, studied the well-being of leaders. What the book's authors found was that "Managers report more stress and burnout, worse work-life balance, and worse physical wellbeing than the individual contributors on the teams they lead." And, as Gallup reported in its State of the American Manager,[15] since leaders account for 70 percent of the variance in their team's engagement, a leader's feelings of overwhelm, stress, and anxiety are almost certain to negatively impact their entire organization's performance. There's a significant trickle-down effect.

Alleviating feelings of stress and overwork are key to being a great leader who sits in the middle chair. Fortunately, there are a number of approaches that can have an impact, from exercise— such as the meditation Dwayne started doing before work—to yoga after work, to eating healthy foods and sleeping at least eight hours a night. Creating a work routine that makes it possible to get all your work done, without offloading everything to others, is also critical.

This is true no matter where you sit in the corporate hierarchy. "Titles and structures maintain order and keep everything running smoothly," says fictional advisor Tommy Flinn in Robin Sharma's *The Leader Who Had No Title,* "for an organization to thrive amid all the turbulence in the business world today, each one of us needs to assume personal responsibility by becoming the CEO of our own roles and leaders within our current positions." Anyone at any level can be a leader. "You don't have to have a title to be a leader," Sharma says. In fact, you can find leaders at every level within an organization.

LEADERS HAVE A GROWTH MINDSET

Emerging leaders can sit in the middle chair, while CEOs may sit in the right or left chairs. Title has nothing to do with which chair people sit in and Anne was a great example of this. An entry-level human resources employee within a mid-sized accounting company, Anne was an emerging leader. She was hungry to learn. She had no formal education but invested her free time in reading every book she could find on the topic, listening to podcasts or magazine articles that others recommended. She immersed herself in learning all she could about human resources, psychology, high performance, and having an impact at work. She was a catalyst for change. She was a *spark*, as Angie Morgan and Courtney Lynch describe in their book by the same name.

As a result of her strong performance and eagerness to learn, Anne was quickly promoted to a manager role. She was a positive force within the organization and people took notice. Employees sought her out for advice and others wanted to work with her. That is the sign of a great leader—when others choose to align with you, whether at work, at school, or in the community. What distinguished Anne from her colleagues was her growth mindset. That is, Anne realized she was born with innate talents, but that those abilities did not represent her full potential.

Anne had discovered what psychologist Angela Duckworth had written about in her book, *Grit*. Duckworth says, "Without effort, your talent is nothing more than unmet potential. Without effort, your skill is nothing more than what you could have done but didn't." As Anne worked to improve her knowledge and experience, she was striving to reach her full potential. Although she didn't have a degree, that didn't mean she would forever be at an educational disadvantage, she understood. Through hard work, she could effectively catch up and even surpass her degreed colleagues.

That's what a growth mindset represents—a belief that it is possible to improve skills, learn entirely new ones, and strengthen weaker abilities, with action. People with a growth mindset recognize that their current skills don't define who they are, or limit what they can do. So they invest time, energy, and effort in adding to them. In contrast, anyone with a fixed mindset believes that no amount of effort will change their basic abilities, and so they don't grow. Or, as Duckworth explains it in *Grit*, "When you keep searching for ways to change your situation for the better, you stand a chance of finding them. When you stop searching, assuming they can't be found, you guarantee they won't." It's a self-fulfilling prophecy. If you believe you can't improve, you don't try, and, consequently, you don't improve.

People in the middle chair have the growth mindset and are gritty. Their attitude is that life doesn't happen to them—they make their life happen. Metaphorically, they are in the driver's seat of their own car. They know where they want to go, take initiative, and step on the gas. When life gets bumpy, with lots of construction and roadblocks, they ask for directions and find a detour. They are hungry to learn skills to improve their life, surround themselves with those who can guide or mentor them, and keep trying when they fail.

Although Anne started out in her new job in the left chair, somewhat self-conscious and unsure of herself in her new role, she was motivated to move to the middle chair. Through her initiative to learn all she could, to remain open to feedback, to seek out middle-chair colleagues to learn from, her confidence grew and self-doubt diminished. As others asked for her input and guidance, she recognized her expanding expertise. She moved to the middle chair and was later promoted.

Her boss proudly said, "Anne does a great job and

THERE'S A SAYING THAT "IQ GETS YOU HIRED, EQ GETS YOU PROMOTED."

everyone loves to work with her." She had the IQ skills and was hungry to continually develop her leadership EQ skills. That's a great leader.

THE IMPORTANCE OF SITTING IN THE MIDDLE CHAIR

Although you likely sit in one of The Three Chairs most of the time, most of us will move to different chairs in different environments. In some situations, you may feel more confident and self-assured, while in other situations you may feel inferior or out of place.

Many CEOs have reported that at work they sit in the middle chair, thanks to their confidence in their business skills, but when they get home, they feel they sit in the left chair—feeling very inadequate with their marriage or parenting skills.

It is very possible that people may perceive you as sitting in the middle chair, but behind the mask, you may relate more to the left or right chair. This happens frequently. We can appear confident, but internally we may be crippled with perfection anxiety or unrealistic expectations, and may be obsessed with what others think of us—all because we have a toxic belief that our self-worth is based on achievement. You may catch yourself doing this if you tell yourself that you're worthy only if you earn a six-figure salary, land the sale you've been pursuing, or get that job you've recently applied for. But achievement should never determine your self-worth—it won't move you toward the middle chair.

Someone in the left or right chair could be highly skilled and have achieved enormous worldly "success," including wealth, status, power, or popularity, and yet still feel unfulfilled, deeply insecure, and unhappy, which is why they don't sit in the middle chair. By the same token, you can be a new employee or a child, feel confident in who you are, and see yourself sitting in the middle chair. Why? Because external achievement does not determine what chair you sit in. It is solely determined by your mindset and attitude.

We can all learn how to become great leaders who sit in the middle chair, regardless of our position, age, ethnicity, education, or any other characteristic. The middle chair is where great leaders sit. It's where people sit who are comfortable in their own skin, because they know their self-worth. They view all people as equal—they don't put themselves or others down. They prioritize their values, goals and self-care, know their skills, are hungry to learn new ones, and easily lift up those around them.

> YOUR SELF-WORTH SHOULD NOT BE DETERMINED BY YOUR NET WORTH.

Chapter 2 Action Steps: Apply the learning! Complete the exercise in *The Three Chairs: Workbook* & *Team Discussion Questions*. Go to www.dkleadership.org/thethreechairs for these bonus tools.

3

BUILDING SELF-LEADERSHIP SKILLS

"We hold ourselves back in ways both big and small,
by lacking self-confidence, by not raising our hands,
and by pulling back when we should be leaning in."

—Sheryl Sandberg, author of *Lean In*

Most people who meet Rachel might presume she is sitting in the middle chair. That's how she is perceived by the outside world. A manager in a growing engineering company, she has a reputation for making things happen, and is certainly a high performer. She's a go-getter. She comes across as put-together and confident—the quintessential leader who occupies the middle chair.

But behind the scenes, Rachel was quickly approaching burnout when I met her. She was becoming overwhelmed with all of her commitments and unsure of what to do to get a handle on her obligations and reduce her anxiety and stress. Her self-confidence was plummeting. In reality, Rachel was sitting between the middle and left chairs. Depending on the task she was completing, the people she was interacting with, or how she was feeling that day, her chair position—her self-confidence—shifted from one to the other.

And that's how we all are, really. No one sits in a particular chair 100 percent of the time. As I shared earlier, The Three Chairs are more like a fluid continuum than three set locations.

In Rachel's case, because she was a self-starter who was skilled at building other people up and getting her work done, she sat in the middle chair a good portion of her day. She was generally confident.

But there were also times—even whole days or weeks—when she sat in the left chair. In particular, she was in the left chair when she said "yes" to too many obligations or responsibilities; she often had difficulty saying "no." Sometimes she said "yes" because of her self-confidence, other times because she underestimated how long a project would take, or even what was required to do a good job. And then she would become anxious and overwhelmed. She felt stressed, weighed down by all the commitments she had made that she was now struggling to live up to, with the result that she was tough and critical towards herself. She was simply wearing too many hats, which wasn't healthy for her.

ROLE-BASED DIFFERENCES IN BURNOUT

Rachel is typical, however. I see a lot of women, in particular, struggle with saying "no" to others. Many have a need to care for others, so they say "yes" even when they really shouldn't, because they barely have time for their own highest priorities. Consequently, they are more likely to experience burnout. As a *Forbes* article[16] explains, "Burnout is more likely when employees expect too much out of themselves, feel inadequate or incompetent..." In other words, when they're sitting in the left chair.

LEADERSHIP STARTS WITH UNDERSTANDING AND MANAGING SELF.

A Montreal University study[17] found that women experience more stress than men, but for different reasons. Women are more likely to burn out at work due to frustration with a lower level of authority and decision-making, while men burn out because of greater difficulty managing their time. But the truth is, people experiencing burnout aren't always the senior level staff members with decision-making power. Workers at every level of an organization are prone to stress and overwhelm. Deloitte's study[18] of burnout found that 77 percent of workers have experienced burnout. The primary drivers of burnout are a lack of support or recognition from leadership, unrealistic deadlines or expectations regarding results, and consistently working long hours, including weekends. Gallup's study[19] of burnout reported similar results. Gallup found that 23 percent of workers surveyed felt burned out always or most of the time, while 44 percent reported feeling burned out some of the time.

STRATEGICALLY MIRROR REFUELING TO AVOID BURNOUT

So how do you avoid burnout? One critical way is to match your investment in your organization or job with your investment in self-care. The more you give of yourself, by staying late at work, helping others, dealing with stressful situations, the more you need to refuel your body and mind. That might mean time off, turning off your cell phone, taking a weekend away—whatever works to replenish your emotional reserves. It may help to visualize this need for renewal and refilling as an ocean wave. In all roles, especially high-performing ones, you need to have an ebb and flow of work and restorative activities.

A common pattern among CEOs, senior leaders, and managers in fast-growing organizations is that if they don't strategically mirror refueling, meaning self-care, their marriages may deteriorate, their kids or teens start acting out, and/or they develop health problems, which adversely impacts their productivity. Self-care is not a suggestion for high-performance—it's a requirement. The more you give, the more you need to refuel—or risk burning out.

Performance psychologist Jim Loehr and Tony Schwartz, authors of *The Power of Full Engagement*, say, "We live in a world that celebrates work and activity, ignores renewal and recovery, and fails to recognize that both are necessary for sustained high performance ... The more exacting the challenge, the more rigorous our rituals need to be."

For Rachel, trying to do it all was damaging her physical and mental health. She needed to delegate more to her team, to give herself time for self-care. When she finally did, she freed up her own schedule and empowered them. It was a win-win. They felt more trusted and challenged, rather than being bored and disengaged. Of course, holding on to as many tasks as possible for herself had become Rachel's *modus operandi*, her personal style. She wasn't intentionally stifling the growth of her employees, but that was the end result nonetheless. Making the decision to delegate more re-energized her team and dramatically reduced her own feelings of stress and danger of burnout—plus, it left time to refuel with her husband and family.

ARIANNA HUFFINGTON, FORMER OWNER OF THE HUFFINGTON POST, HAD HER OWN EPIPHANY REGARDING BURNOUT THANKS TO A SCARY INCIDENT BACK IN 2007. SHE WAS WORKING FROM HOME AND SUDDENLY PASSED OUT, REGAINING CONSCIOUSNESS A SHORT WHILE LATER TO DISCOVER SHE WAS BLEEDING PROFUSELY FROM HER FACE, DUE TO A CUT OVER HER EYE AND A BROKEN CHEEKBONE. MEDICAL TESTS REVEALED SHE WAS COMPLETELY EXHAUSTED. IT WAS THE "WAKE-UP CALL THAT CHANGED MY LIFE," HUFFINGTON HAS SAID.

TO BE A GREAT LEADER, YOU NEED TO TAKE CARE OF YOURSELF AS MUCH AS YOU TAKE CARE OF OTHERS.

THE 5 LEADERSHIP EQ SKILLS™

Rachel was using several leadership skills to move to the middle chair. By focusing first on self-care (Stress-Management Skills), this gave her capacity to prioritize and delegate (Decision-Making Skills) and spend her time communicating and building her team dynamic (Communication and Relationship Skills). To sit in the middle chair consistently, you need to be able to effectively manage yourself and others, which requires many different skills. It all goes back to emotional intelligence, or EQ. Great leaders have it and the good news is that you can, too. As I shared earlier, I've identified five core skills that I call The 5 Leadership EQ Skills™ which are represented by the acronym CARDS™:

- C = Communication Skills

- A = Attitude and Goal-Setting Skills

- R = Relationship Skills

- D = Decision-Making, Time Management, and Self-Discipline Skills

- S = Stress, Anxiety, and Emotion Management Skills

These five CARDS™ determine the degree to which an individual is behaving like a great leader. I have noticed that when I coach middle managers or senior leaders, it is often communication, stress, or lack of emotion management skills due to poor self-care that causes them the most pain and derails their productivity. And when I coach emerging leaders, it's often their lack of confidence, goal-setting shaped by perfectionism, decision-making, and time management skills that cause a lot of angst. Regardless, all great leaders across all levels who consistently sit in the middle chair have effectively mastered all five CARDS™. So, while you may have strong skills in one or two of these areas, to become a great leader, you'll want to work on strengthening all five.

Specifically, here are The 5 Leadership EQ Skills™ of great leaders who sit in the middle chair that you should focus on developing:

Communication skills. Great leaders need strong two-way communication skills. That is, they need to be able to share information as well as to receive and process it from others. People with high emotional intelligence give feedback effectively, inspire change, and increase their ability to influence others with each interaction. They also are eager for feedback and are able to receive it with an attitude of humility, rather than defensiveness. They are hungry to improve and they value others' input. They try to create a safe environment for others so that issues can be discussed. They don't shy away from conflict, but rather, lean into it, and focus on solving problems quickly, not blaming others or avoiding issues. They take ownership for their part in conflict. They understand that thriving teams will have conflict and see it as an opportunity to learn. As Patrick Lencioni wrote in *The Advantage: Why Organizational Health Trumps Everything Else in Business,* "When there is trust, conflict becomes nothing but the pursuit of truth, an attempt to find the best possible answer."

Attitude and goal-setting skills. Your attitude includes how you think about yourself, your overall self-esteem, and your ability to set goals as a result. Someone with high emotional intelligence, who sits in the middle chair, is confident, aware of their strengths, and can recognize and acknowledge their weaknesses. They set meaningful-yet-achievable goals for themselves, pursue excellence and not perfection, and are willing to ask others for help in order to reach their goals. They know asking for support does not indicate weakness. Carol Dweck, author of *Mindset: The New Psychology of Success,* says, "True self-confidence is the courage to be open—to welcome change and new ideas regardless of their source. Real self-confidence is not reflected in a title, an expensive suit, a fancy car, or a series of acquisitions. It is reflected in your mindset: your readiness to grow."

Relationship skills. Individuals with high emotional intelligence, who sit in the middle chair, work hard to understand others, including understanding their differences. This interest in others and desire to understand fosters powerful relationships with team members, which leads to strong team dynamics, which results in higher engagement, productivity, and a positive corporate culture. This type of individual tries to see situations from other people's point of view. This is where seeking to understand the differences in generation, gender, culture, race, and personality (among others) is important. Someone with high emotional intelligence understands that people are different, have unique experiences, and interpret the world differently. High-EQ people are also givers: they look for opportunities to lift people up; they build authentic relationships with those around them; as a result, people want to work with and for them. As author Adam Grant said in *Give and Take: A Revolutionary Approach to Success,* "This is what I find most magnetic about successful givers: they get to the top without cutting others down, finding ways of expanding the pie that benefit themselves and the people around them."

Decision-making, time management, and self-discipline skills. People with high emotional intelligence, who sit in the middle chair, have a well-developed ability to set priorities. With that skill, they also manage their time efficiently, make decisions according to their values, and stay focused on taking initiative toward their goals. They understand boundaries—why we need them for high performance, how to set them, and how to stand by them. They are clear about when they should say "yes" and "no" to protect their highest priorities. They are highly self-disciplined. As best-selling author Brian Tracy says in *No Excuses! The Power Of Self-Discipline,* "You can make excuses or you can make progress. You choose."

Stress, anxiety, and emotion management skills. Leaders with high emotional intelligence, who sit in the middle chair, understand how emotions work and know how to manage change. They know what they feel—meaning they can label their feelings, understand why they feel it (which is a harder skill to master), and, most importantly, instead of venting and blaming, they direct their energy toward taking action steps based on what they learned. Doing so reduces their anxiety and stress, which enables them to improve their focus and communication style. Similarly, author Travis Bradberry writes in *Emotional Intelligence 2.0*, "Understand why you do the things you do, the better equipped you'll be to keep your emotions from running the show." Essentially, great leaders manage their emotions, rather than letting their emotions manage them.

Great leadership starts with self—i.e., before you try to lead anyone else, you need to effectively lead yourself. Don't know where to begin? Start on self-awareness and building The 5 Leadership EQ Skills™. Understanding yourself is powerful and you need this data to effectively delegate and lead others.

Chapter 3 Action Steps: Apply the learning! Complete the exercise in *The Three Chairs: Workbook & Team Discussion Questions*. Go to www.dkleadership.org/thethreechairs for these bonus tools.

4

LEARNING TO LEAD OTHERS

"If you want the cooperation of humans around you,
you must make them feel they are important—and
you do that by being genuine and humble."

—Nelson Mandela, former President of South Africa

few years ago, I concluded a keynote speech in front
of a large audience and was immediately pulled aside
by the sponsoring company's CEO. He wanted me to
coach one of their rising star professionals who was being considered for a promotion. He was a skilled financier, currently in
a director role, but his promotion to vice president was in jeop-
ardy because no one wanted to work with him. His employer
wanted to convey their concerns to him but didn't know how
to articulate the issue. After hearing my presentation about The
Three Chairs, he asked for my help.

This story is one I hear often. People often get promoted
because they have the required technical skills (IQ), but since
they don't sit in the middle chair and lack the needed people
skills (EQ), no one wants to work with them. Consequently,
their teams struggle with engagement, productivity, and
retention.

George, the talented financier the CEO spoke of, was clearly sitting in the right chair, which his bosses understood immediately upon hearing me describe The Three Chairs. He was great at his job but because of his attitude, he came across as arrogant and demanding. They knew he would never be a great leader until he learned how to sit in the middle chair. He needed a coach to help him identify his own leadership style—one that would attract other high performers rather than repel them— because his current style just wasn't working. He was a perfectionist with extremely high standards, to which he held himself as well as others. Unfortunately, George's standards were simply unattainable, yet he insisted everyone he worked with meet or exceed them. This created a toxic work atmosphere that no one wanted to be in.

Of course, you can't be a great leader if you have no one willing to work alongside you. Being a great leader is inspiring others to follow you because they want to, not because they need to or are required to by their job description. His CEO, vice presidents, and I set up a meeting to explain the situation to him, hoping for a positive outcome.

We were all pleasantly surprised by his reaction. Rather than being defensive, he wholeheartedly embraced the coaching offered. George had excellent self-awareness, so his assessment of his strengths, which included being focused, self-disciplined, and detailed, were accurate. He also recognized his weaknesses, which were that he was critical, demanding, and a perfectionist. Yet he had no clue what to do about those weaknesses—what adjustments he needed to make, or how. He seemed relieved when offered coaching. Because he is so achievement-oriented, George quickly grasped that he wouldn't progress any further in his company unless he was coached in adopting essential behavior changes. He understood the cost to his career of not changing and was highly motivated to get started on learning how to become a great leader. He was an ideal client.

We began working together with a plan to meet every two to three weeks. His first task was to ask for specific feedback from the two vice presidents to whom he reported, in order to set his own goals for improvement and to get a baseline measurement to track his progress. The first couple of months we worked on his interactions with others and he learned new language to use when talking to members of his team, in person and email. When we discussed these approaches, he admitted that he hadn't really thought about how his words impacted others. He had never put himself in their shoes. He was so intent on communicating what *he* needed that he hadn't considered whether his words or tone were too harsh; he didn't think it really mattered as long as he got his point across. But he quickly recognized what a difference it did make.

THE POWER OF PRAISE

During the second month of George's coaching, I encouraged him to speak up when a direct report did a good job—to tell them directly. If something needed to get worked on or tweaked, let them know that, too. But first let them know what they did well, to reinforce the positive behavior.

George thought this sounded a lot like coddling or babying them, which is a common objection, but I explained that encouraging them and relaying clear instructions reinforces what you want them to continue doing *and* what needs to be changed. It takes only a few minutes and saves enormous emotional energy and time required to clear up misunderstandings later, plus it builds a positive working environment, I assured him. It's one of the simplest, most time-efficient habits of great leaders that helps team members feel inspired, coached, listened to—and it's free!

Although it felt awkward at first, George agreed to try and was pleasantly surprised by the reactions he received. He saw a change almost immediately, especially with his millennial team members, who beamed whenever he acknowledged the great work they had completed. He told me that the first time he acknowledged the good work of one of his direct reports, it was so uncomfortable for him that he couldn't make eye contact and just stared at his computer, stuttering his words to voice a few words of praise. In that moment, the emotional energy slightly shifted in their dynamic to be more positive and open. The team member just stared blankly at him, shocked at receiving acknowledgment, since she usually only heard silence or criticism. The next day she took the initiative, which she seldom did, to ask George if there was anything she could take off of his plate. Then he was speechless! How George treated her had inspired her to want to follow him.

George was starting to understand what author Simon Sinek said in *Leaders Eat Last: Why Some Teams Pull Together and Others Don't:* "When a leader embraces their responsibility to care for people instead of caring for numbers, then people will follow..." Having the courage to voice authentic affirmation, and not just think it, when great work is done, is one way that leaders can show they care for their people.

The desire for ongoing positive and constructive feedback is a popular request from millennials. One reason is that many have been raised with regular feedback from parents, teachers, and coaches, and now they highly value the same from employers but aren't necessarily receiving it. Part of the reason for the lack of feedback may be that boomers balk at this demand for constant acknowledgment; they find it irritating to have to provide it, despite the fact that feedback is one of the best ways to help their team members grow. Receiving feedback is one of the fastest ways to build emotional intelligence, so it's good news that millennials are asking for it. World renowned psychologist Daniel Goleman[20] says, "Feedback works best if you ask people whose opinions you value and trust ... this information is immensely valuable for developing further strengths in EI, because it gives you a view of yourself you can never get on your own."

THE FEEDBACK WE WANT TO RECEIVE

Great leaders don't just give praise; they *are* more likely to give honest, direct feedback to others and are also open to receiving feedback about their performance. They welcome input.

As Brené Brown says in *Dare to Lead: Brave Work. Tough Conversations. Whole Hearts,* "We have to be able to take feedback—regardless of how it's delivered—and apply it productively. We have to do this for a simple reason: Mastery requires feedback. I don't care what we're trying to master—and whether we're trying to develop greatness or proficiency—it always requires feedback."

People in the left chair are often afraid to give feedback, or to receive it. They're so afraid of hurting someone's feelings, or upsetting them, that they avoid sharing any information that might lead to a confrontation. They also don't want to receive feedback that may challenge their intellect or abilities. In contrast, people in the right chair often have no problem voicing their feedback. The problem is that they often voice it with criticism, arrogance, and without empathy. Learning how to receive and give feedback effectively, so the person hears it and is inspired to do something with it, is a skill of great leaders in the middle chair.

A *Harvard Business Review* study[21] conducted by Jack Zenger and Joseph Folkman found that 57 percent of employees said they would rather receive corrective feedback than positive feedback from their employers. That statistic aligns with another question, which reported that 72 percent of employees said they thought their performance would improve if they received corrective feedback from their managers. Meaning, the reason more employees crave corrective feedback is that they see it as a path to performance improvement; without it, they don't know what they can do to improve.

WHAT CAN YOU DO TO ATTRACT FOLLOWERS?

Becoming a great leader, sitting in the middle chair, begins with encouraging others to be their best. But it boils down to a number of small communication skills that, together, have a major impact on the willingness of others to follow you. Let's look at some ways that will earn fans and attract followers for all levels of leaders:

- **Affirm team members**. Don't hold back from genuinely praising team members on their performance. It makes them feel valued and appreciated, which leads to higher engagement and loyalty.

- **Offer constructive feedback in private**. There's a saying that praise should be shared publicly and problems privately. If you have anything that could be construed or interpreted as negative to share with a team member, take them aside quietly to convey your corrective feedback. This allows them to process the information without feeling exposed or embarrassed. It also shows that you want to protect their feelings and reputation, which makes them feel safe.

- **Be open to feedback.** Understand that you have strengths and areas to work on, too. No one is perfect. When you receive constructive feedback, try not to get defensive. Listen to the data, don't personalize it. Try to learn from it to improve your performance.

- **Ask for feedback from people at work and home.** Realize many people are uncomfortable offering their honest thoughts, so lean in and ask for it so you can hear their perspective and seek excellence in all parts of your life.

- **Acknowledge the career potential you see in team members.** Verbalizing to members of your team that you see they have tremendous potential for success in your organization boosts their self-confidence and morale. It also makes them more loyal. While complimenting them on their performance and potential, lay out a potential career path for them, to help them visualize what they might aspire to do or be.

Put these skills together and you are on your way to becoming a great leader sitting in the middle chair. But without them, it will be a struggle. My client Lee discovered that the hard way, as you will see next.

FACING IMPOSTER SYNDROME

One of my very first organizational clients was Lee, an extremely gifted manager of a large non-profit organization. She had graduated at the top of her class in her MBA program, was a very hard worker, and was looking forward to being promoted to a senior leadership role after a position opened up. However, Lee was sitting in the left chair, mainly because she felt like a fraud. She wasn't sure she deserved the success she had achieved. Because of her arrogant behavior, however, those around her thought she was in the right chair. She thought she was a shoo-in for the promotion, due to her years of hard work and dedication, and was devastated when it was announced that a younger, less experienced employee was getting the job. That was a huge wake-up call for Lee.

Fortunately, rather than just sulking and complaining, she took the opportunity to examine why she was passed over, to determine what she could do to make sure she got it the next time. What Lee soon realized was that she was the problem. She had a toxic mindset about herself that pushed her to expect too much of herself and others.

Like George, Lee was a perfectionist. She had unreasonably high expectations for everyone, with all-or-nothing thinking—something was either perfect or it wasn't. There was no grey area, no "good enough" with her; hence, she was argumentative and critical of others' efforts, which is why no one liked working with her. There was no upside. If you did a good job, it still wouldn't be good enough for Lee so, instead of getting praise, you'd hear all the revisions Lee wanted to be made ASAP.

THE PATH FORWARD

When we started working together, Lee began by recognizing the toxic view she had of herself. Her behavior was due to feeling that she was not worthy, that she wasn't good enough, and that she had to be perfect to justify having her job. We took a two-pronged approach to changing how she viewed herself and her situation:

- **Get feedback**. Lee needed to find out exactly why she didn't get the job. What skills did she lack? What skills should she develop to be in contention for the next opening? I encouraged her to set up a meeting with her boss and get specific feedback, but she resisted doing so because she wanted only to hide, where she felt safe and comfortable. So I coached her that if her value is ambition and her goal was to get the next promotion, she needed to face the issues and lean in. Yes, she would feel scared and uncomfortable, and she needed to do it anyway. Never let a feeling like comfort make a decision, I advised her. Feelings are very powerful and important to listen to, but when it comes to decision-making, you need to make the final decision based on values, principles, and goals—not feelings.

- **Mindset shift**. On top of figuring out a game plan for earning a promotion, Lee had to work on her mindset. She had to stop thinking that she had to be perfect; she needed to replace that mindset with healthier thinking. No, it's not easy, but it *is* possible.

Although work on her mindset was the second area Lee focused on, it was and is the most important—for everyone. Your mindset is where the power is—the power to change your life.

When leaders are encouraging, give direct and honest ongoing feedback that is both positive and constructive to their teams, have a healthy mindset, set realistic expectations of excellence rather than perfection, and humbly ask for feedback to learn how they can improve, they create an environment, a culture of emotional safety, where team members feel they can be themselves and can thrive.

That is exactly what Google's Project Aristotle research found, which studied the commonalities across highly effective teams, and discovered that the biggest determinant of a high-performing team is psychological safety, or fostering an environment where every member can be themselves with each other. A *New York Times* article[22] on the study summarized:

> "What Project Aristotle has taught people within Google is that no one wants to put on a "work face" when they get to the office. No one wants to leave part of their personality and inner life at home. But to be fully present at work, to feel "psychologically safe," we must know that we can be free enough, sometimes, to share the things that scare us without fear of recriminations. We must be able to talk about what is messy or sad, to have hard conversations with colleagues who are driving us crazy. We can't be focused just on efficiency."

TO EFFECTIVELY LEAD OTHERS, YOU NEED TO CREATE AN ENVIRONMENT OF SAFETY—WHERE PEOPLE CAN BE THEMSELVES, LET THEIR GUARD DOWN AND HAVE THE COURAGE TO HAVE CRUCIAL CONVERSATIONS WITH THEIR TEAM.

The stories of George and Lee were similar—neither had created a team environment of emotional safety. Both received feedback that they were critical and difficult to work with, and as a result, no one wanted to work with them. They were both perfectionists—a standard they had for themselves and those around them—which was impossible to achieve. The result? A negative, draining culture, where team members' guards were up, and no one felt safe to talk about real issues that needed discussing.

Fortunately, both leaders were hungry to learn. They realized there was a problem, since both were stressed, unhappy, missing career advancements, and embarrassed their teams didn't want to work with them. They just needed a few concrete tools to help.

George started focusing on giving more ongoing positive feedback to his team. But he qualified that agreement with, "I will do it, Karyn, but only when it's earned. I'm not giving fluffy praise," he told me, and he was right to take that approach, since praise needs to be authentic and specific in order to be effective.

While Lee worked on changing her mindset from perfection to excellence, for both herself and her team, this new mindset and realistic goal focused on achievement, not perfection, helped her be more relaxed in her mood and in her communication with others. Lee also sought feedback from those she worked with, but she took it one step further: she asked her husband and teens for their feedback, too. Getting both professional and personal feedback is often extremely useful, since families can be ruthless with honest insight. All of these action steps, done on a regular basis, began to shift their team culture and create a sense of safety for both George and Lee. George was promoted four months later to vice president, and Lee was promoted to senior leader within nine months. They both had the IQ skills; they just needed to develop some of The 5 Leadership EQ Skills™ to help them move towards the middle chair.

Chapter 4 Action Steps: Apply the learning! Complete the exercise in *The Three Chairs: Workbook* & *Team Discussion Questions*. Go to www.dkleadership.org/thethreechairs for these bonus tools.

PART II

BUILDING CORE SKILLS OF GREAT LEADERS

Since great leadership is learned, everyone has the potential to become a great leader. It doesn't matter your background, your education, or your career experience thus far—you can develop new skills that will make you a great leader, if you are hungry to learn and have a mindset to grow.

Leadership is a huge topic. There are many ways to approach it and study it. We focus specifically on the niche of emotional intelligence (EQ) as the key to becoming a great leader. As mentioned previously, we encourage the development of five core skills for all levels of leaders—from emerging leaders, to managers, to senior leaders. Let's dive more deeply into those core skills in the following five chapters.

5

COMMUNICATION SKILLS

"Communication is a skill that you can learn. It's like riding a bicycle or typing. If you're willing to work at it, you can rapidly improve the quality of every part of your life."

—Brian Tracy, author

Remember Dwayne from chapter 1—the high-performing CEO who was getting burned out due to overwhelm? We worked together to create an entirely new daily routine, one that would give him time for his highest level of performance and time to refuel. Daily routines are game-changers and required for effective communication.

This simple redesign of Dwayne's day "changed my life," he told me and his senior leadership team, because of the positive ripple effect. Building in time for himself gave him balance, calm, and made it possible for him to listen better—to his staff members, clients, colleagues, and family. Self-care is critical because it affects our emotions, which impacts our communication. Research published in the *Journal of Personality and Social Psychology*[23] underscore this phenomenon, reporting that people with positive affect have higher quality communication and interaction with others.

THE TRUST-COMMUNICATION LINK

Honest, transparent communication, voiced with kindness, builds trust. The right chair is often honest and direct, but without kindness. The left chair is often kind, but not fully honest, because information is held back to avoid conflict. The middle chair is both honest and kind, and that's the difference. When someone tells you something that is accurate with kindness, and clearly tells you what you can do to improve the situation—focusing on the solution not the problem—your trust in them naturally rises. Research published in *Personnel Review*[24] reported that managers who are provided guidance on how to improve, who are open to ideas, and who are skilled problem solvers, build trust more easily in their business relationships.

Trust in relationships builds over time. The longer you work alongside someone, the more you can gauge how trustworthy they are. Trust is built or destroyed based on actions. When a person's actions and words are congruent and aligned, meaning what they say is what they do, your trust increases.

Keep in mind that there's a difference between trusting a person's skill, or IQ, and trusting a person's character, or EQ. We can trust that someone is capable of doing a job (IQ), yet still question whether they are honest, and/or will take initiative or responsibility (EQ).

> WHEN A PERSON'S ACTIONS AND WORDS ARE CONGRUENT AND ALIGNED (WHAT THEY SAY IS WHAT THEY DO), OUR TRUST INCREASES.

RESPONDING TO LEADERS WHO AREN'T SITTING IN THE MIDDLE CHAIR

Daniel is a brilliant leader for a growing insurance company. He is well-respected and held up as a role model for other leaders. From afar, he looks like he has it all together—like he's sitting in the middle chair. Until you work with him.

Although Daniel appears to everyone outside his organization to sit in the middle chair, anyone who works with him recognizes that he actually leads from the right chair. He belittles his staff, is incredibly critical of them in public, frequently yells at them to make a point, and piles on work without thought or regard for what has already been assigned. As a result of his leadership style, he has created a culture of anxiety. His team members are constantly walking on eggshells for fear of upsetting him.

I was called in to work with Daniel and his team, to help them create a healthier team dynamic together. Instead of focusing specifically on Daniel, which would have made him very defensive and disengaged if that was the starting point, we started by talking about The Three Chairs as a practical leadership framework. This helped get everyone on the same page, created alignment, and showed how great leaders and teams function in their communication. From there we discussed healthy new "rules" for great leaders who sit in the middle chair.

Once you establish the rules, team members can hold each other accountable to this higher standard. It was easy to explain how each person should respond if team members are sitting in the right or left chair. For example, I explained that all leaders— from emerging leaders to managers to senior leaders—who are sitting in the right chair need to be dealt with directly. When an issue or conflict arises, they need to be made aware of it right away, in private. Hold each other accountable and raise concerns respectfully. Leaders in the right chair will have more respect for those who respond assertively; they see that type of behavior as a sign of strength. Being "respectfully direct" is the best course of action.

In addition, if you want to be a great leader, you need to not only raise concerns, but also have the courage to problem-solve. Just talking about problems is not going to create progress. To build great teams that drive engagement and productivity, leaders need to develop strong, assertive communication and problem-solving skills.

Daniel was frustrated with his disengaged team, and his team members were fed up with the anxious team culture he had created. While their starting place was different, they were all eager to make the situation better and learn new tools.

> "RELATIONAL SKILLS ARE THE MOST IMPORTANT ABILITIES IN LEADERSHIP."
> JOHN C. MAXWELL
> BESTSELLING AUTHOR OF
> *DEVELOPING THE LEADERS AROUND YOU: HOW TO HELP OTHERS REACH THEIR FULL POTENTIAL*

We started by taking two steps. First, team members made a list of "unresolved issues" and prioritized them from most important to least important. Second, Daniel and his entire team learned new assertiveness tools to start discussing and problem-solving the issues together. As author Patrick Lencioni said in *The Five Dysfunctions of a Team,* "Great teams do not hold back with one another. They are unafraid to air their dirty laundry. They admit their mistakes, their weaknesses, and their concerns without fear of reprisal."

Creating a safe place for Daniel and his team members to take this two-stepped approach was extremely effective. Team members were able to start talking assertively about issues that had been piling up over months and years—a "traffic jam" of

> THE BUREAU OF LABOR STATISTICS[25] REPORTS THAT A TYPICAL MANAGER SPENDS 25-40 PERCENT OF THEIR TIME HANDLING WORKPLACE CONFLICTS.

unresolved issues—and were able to begin focusing on problem solving. There were heated moments and even some tears— one team member vulnerably shared how the stress at work was impacting her marriage— but, in the end, there was significant insight, understanding, growth, and progress. They focused on the most important, time-sensitive topics first, with a razor-sharp focus on solving problems.

THE IMPORTANCE OF ASSERTIVENESS

As we have noted, assertive communication is the most effective approach with leaders, no matter which chair they're sitting in, actually. Allowing conflicts to fester by not addressing them only fosters workplace drama that can kill productivity. It's such a waste of time. Adopting a problem-solving mindset and communicating directly with everyone is the only way to encourage progress and improvement, but especially with leaders sitting in the right chair.

During my doctoral studies in Pennsylvania, I learned the "Burger Technique," also known as the "Sandwich Technique," as a practical assertiveness tool to give feedback. To be honest, I didn't like it initially. I thought it sounded fake, awkward, ineffective, and manipulative, until I started to use it. It was then that I saw how powerful it could be when used appropriately— the key phrase being *could be*; I've seen many people use it ineffectively. Like riding a bike, it's awkward, wobbly at the beginning, but with a lot of practice and trial-and-error, the "Burger Technique" can become an effective way to give feedback.

Basically, this approach involves sandwiching constructive feedback, which is sometimes construed as negative or what needs improvement, between two positive statements; one of my clients calls it the "shit sandwich." He had learned the technique during his MBA studies but never liked it either, until he heard me explain the power of the tool when used correctly.

Here is how it works: You start with something complimentary, i.e., that the person is genuinely doing well. Then you take responsibility for anything that is your part in the issue that has come up, and wrap up with mention of intent, to explain why you're sharing this information. In the middle is the meat of the matter—the behavior that has to change or the need that is not being met. Here is an overview and some sample phrases:

Positive and Take Responsibility (Share two or three actions that the person is doing well and anything for which you should take responsibility):

- *"I appreciate..."* or *"Thank you for..."*

- *"I take responsibility that I should have..."*

Growth Area (Share the specific action you want them to do next time. Stick to only one or two meats. Keep it short and to-the-point):

- *"I need" or "I would appreciate if you could ..."*

- *"I think" or "I feel"*

- *"From my perspective" or "In my opinion"*

Positive Intent and Seek Feedback (Share with them why you are having this conversation and ask for their thoughts in order to start a discussion):

- *"I'm bringing this up because..."*

- *"I really want to solve this together. What are your thoughts on what I've shared?"*

It's simple, time-efficient, and can be—depending on the user's words, body language, tone, and demeanor—extremely effective for addressing issues.

A law firm reached out to me to help them with their communication. Similar to Daniel's group, I had the team write out their list of unresolved communication "traffic jams" and then taught them the "Burger Technique." They appreciated how simple and sequential this tool was. Then they tried it with each other on low-risk topics. Here is what one employee, Simone, shared with her colleague:

(Positive and Taking Responsibility) *"Cole, I appreciate you taking on these two accounts for me. This has been super helpful, since my workload has been full the last few weeks. I realize I should have spent more time going over my expectations, so next time I'm going to block off time for this. I so appreciate your help!* **(Growth Area)** *Moving forward, could you tweak two things: (1) Copy me on your communication email, just with these two clients this next month, so I know where things stand when I take back the accounts* *and (2) I think these clients are really intuitive with tone in emails. Instead of using the word "you," I think it would be better to say "I" when you email your suggestions.* (**Positive Intent and Seek Feedback**) *Your suggestions are fantastic and I want to make sure they hear them and don't get defensive. What are your thoughts? Is there anything you would like me to do differently?"*

The result? Cole received the feedback well. Why? Because Simone, who had a reputation for being critical, was finally verbalizing *authentic* affirmations with specific solutions and not just criticizing. This encouraged Cole to listen more to what he needed to work on. They were both extremely hard workers, dedicated to the company, and this tool gave them a framework to deal with issues head on, and make progress.

Including positive *authentic* affirmations along with more specific details is important, so that the recipient actually hears what you've shared. Research published in the *Journal of Managerial Psychology*[26] found that while many employees have a negative reaction to receiving feedback, it is often due to how it is delivered. However, when employees know that the feedback is given from a credible

TO BECOME MORE COMFORTABLE VOICING YOUR OWN OPINION—ASSERTING YOURSELF—START PRACTICING WITH EASY PROBLEMS IN LOW-RISK, HIGH-TRUST ENVIRONMENTS. WHEN I WAS TRAINING A GROUP OF SENIOR LEADERS IN COLORADO THESE ASSERTIVENESS SKILLS, I ASKED THEM TO PRACTICE IN TEAMS WITH A REAL EXAMPLE. ALMOST ALL OF THEM CHOSE EXAMPLES FROM HOME. WHY? LIKE LEARNING ANY NEW SKILL, IT'S IMPORTANT TO START EASY AND MOVE TOWARD MORE DIFFICULT. AND FOR MANY PEOPLE, IT'S OFTEN EASIER TO BE ASSERTIVE WITH YOUR SPOUSE OR KIDS THAN WITH YOUR COLLEAGUES OR BOSS.

source in a caring and considerate way, they are more likely to want to improve their performance. If people don't feel cared for, they are less likely to listen to what you have to say and your message won't yield the desired result.

So how can you start developing this assertive, middle-chair communication skill? If you're not comfortable yet delivering constructive feedback in person, you can deliver it via email to start. However, I strongly—*strongly*—recommend getting a confidential third person, such as a coach or mentor who is an effective communicator that you trust, to take a quick read and provide honest feedback *before* you send it. Email is a great way to start developing this skill but, and this is a big warning, the challenge is that email has no nonverbal cues. The recipient can't always pick up on the tone you're intending, so be extremely careful with words to make sure a healthy, respectful tone is coming through. In addition, look for opportunities to stretch your skills with face-to-face interactions for giving feedback; start with low-risk conversations with people who already trust you.

TIMING IS ESSENTIAL

One of the important tricks to effective communication is timing. You may have developed all the right tools, but choosing the wrong time risks escalating the situation. Any constructive feedback needs to be shared in private, and, ideally, when both people have time to talk and their mood is neutral to positive. When we're in a bad mood, it's hard to receive and process more negative news, so wait until you're both able to take in the information in the helpful spirit in which it's offered.

Positive feedback and recognition, on the other hand, can be shared privately or publicly. Why? Because it makes people feel appreciated and valued, and it reinforces the positive culture.

This was never clearer than at an investing company I worked with. I was hired to present a virtual keynote during the pandemic and had the opportunity to watch as the CEO spoke to the organization first. She was so affirming and empathetic, voicing her praise to specific team members in front of the 300-member virtual audience, all of whom were navigating the uncertainty around working from home. The response from the employees was equally appreciative of her message, saying things like, "Thank you for valuing us," "This is the best place to work," "I feel so cared for," and "We need more leaders like you."

THE START OF COMMUNICATION BOUNDARIES™

Great leaders, sitting in the middle chair, establish and convey clear boundaries for communication to help manage expectations. That is, they explain what, when, and how information can and should be relayed to others. The five most effective communication boundaries—represented by the acronym **START**—are the following:

1: Solution-Focused. Great leaders get to the point and focus on solving problems, not wasting time blaming and discussing the issue repeatedly. They listen, get to the point right away, and stay on one topic so that it can be resolved. As Tony Robbins says, "Leaders spend 5 percent of their time on the problem and 95 percent of their time on the solution. Get over it and crush it!"

2: Time to Talk. Great leaders clarify to their team their expectations regarding the timing of information-sharing. When they delegate tasks, they give a deadline for response, so that the recipient knows whether the work needs to be done immediately, or if they have until, say, Friday to provide a deliverable. If you have an important conversation, ask the person when they have time to talk. Be direct and ask, rather than putting off a tough conversation until the last possible minute.

3: Assertive Words. Great leaders also make it clear which words are preferred and which should never be used. Maybe your company refers to vendors as partners, or employees as associates, for example. And maybe you've been told that swearing in front of customers is never acceptable. Those kinds of communication boundaries need to be established. In addition, great leaders focus on assertive language like "I think," "I need," "From my perspective." They stand up for themselves while respecting others. They use the "Burger Technique" when giving feedback, and they take ownership of their part.

4: Restricted and Confidential. Great leaders make clear which pieces of information are confidential, which can be shared within the organization, and which should not leave the room. They identify with whom the information can be shared, setting up a metaphorical fence around details to make it clear who can know what.

5: Triangles, Not (1:1). Great leaders do not create "triangles," also referred to as "triangulation." An article in *Forbes*[27] describes triangulation as "a manipulation tactic that's used when a person is uncomfortable (for whatever reason) about communicating directly with another person about something he is upset about." Instead, they tell a third party. For example, if Ashley is upset with Bruno, she'll avoid him and, instead, tells Max, who has nothing to do with the situation. These communication "triangles" are toxic within workplaces because problems remain frozen and people get involved who have nothing to do with the situation. Great leaders do not create triangles. They deal with situations directly and one-on-one, or together as an entire team. Most human resource managers (HR) are likely nodding right now, because they are often part of the triangle. When team members lack communication skills, they often unload to HR.

Great leaders, sitting in the middle chair, develop their communication skills (**C**ARDS™). They prioritize self-care to build their capacity to communicate more effectively, build trust by ensuring their words and actions match, use the "Burger Technique" to give feedback and problem solve, and use The

START of Communication Boundaries™ as a framework for thriving team communication.

Chapter 5 Action Steps: Apply the learning! Complete the exercise in *The Three Chairs: Workbook* & *Team Discussion Questions.* Go to www.dkleadership.org/thethreechairs for these bonus tools.

6

ATTITUDE AND GOAL-SETTING SKILLS

"Set realistic goals, keep re-evaluating, and be consistent."

—Tennis superstar Venus Williams

Sunny first came to me for help in communicating with her senior team. Two of her team members had abruptly quit, which had shaken her confidence. She also wanted coaching to improve her relationship with her teen daughter, with whom she was having a lot of arguments. She was looking for practical tools that she could apply to both work and family parts of her life. Sunny was frustrated and finally recognized it was time to get some guidance. Looking back, I know that must have been very difficult for her to admit, because Sunny was flipping between the left and right chairs.

To the outside world, Sunny was a successful third-generation family business owner. She had inherited the profitable company in their small town from her father. She was an only child with a passion for business. Externally, she appeared confident and self-assured, but internally, I quickly discovered, she was incredibly critical of herself and those around her. She had high anxiety, high expectations, and imposter syndrome, which was causing a lot of problems at work and at home.

As she described her many insecurities, which she covered up with a tough exterior, I could see the lightbulbs start to go on. She viewed the world in terms of all-or-nothing thinking—there was no grey area. She would set a huge goal she couldn't possibly achieve and then beat herself up when she didn't get it. She put enormous pressure on herself for "carrying" the family business and family legacy. Everyone in their community knew who she was. She employed a large number of the town's population. "People rely on me," she often said, which she then internalized as, "There is no room for error." She was heavily burdened.

As she described her anxiety, she started telling me about her daughter. In doing so, it slowly dawned on Sunny that she was also describing herself. Her daughter had high anxiety, perfectionist tendencies, and her grades were "never good enough." Sunny suddenly realized that, in many ways, her daughter was mirroring her own toxic thinking, which was contributing to their conflict.

When I got Sunny to dig in to uncover her thought pattern, we identified many toxic thoughts, three of which were:

1. *I think I have to be perfect—there is no room to make any mistakes.*

2. *I think my father would be disappointed in me right now.*

3. *I think I am undeserving of my CEO role. I inherited it, I didn't earn it.*

As we peeled back the layers, most of Sunny's thoughts started with "I think"—one sign that it's the powerful narrative, story, attitude, and mindset that we tell ourselves. As a result, she was feeling unworthy, anxious, insecure, and fearful. These unpleasant feelings were impacting all parts of her life at work and home.

At work, she was abrupt, critical, and demanding to her senior team, which led to members abruptly quitting. She was having difficulty making decisions and concentrating. She set unrealistically high goals that were unattainable. Morale was low. Teams were disengaged.

Sunny's home life mirrored her work environment. Her daughter was disengaged, staying in her room and avoiding her mother at all costs in order to avoid arguments. She described her relationship with her husband of 18 years as "roommates" and "distant." She was snappy and critical to everyone around her. She was having difficulty sleeping and starting to drink a lot at night. Her life was in a downward spiral.

You can't directly control how you feel, but you can change how you think, which is part of a domino effect that will shift your behavior. How you think affects how you feel, which affects how you behave. It's important to pay attention to how you feel, and then shift your attention, time and energy to work on what's in your head. The mind is powerful and sophisticated. You cannot simply erase negative thoughts, but you can strategically create new healthy thoughts to replace toxic thoughts. That can then change how you feel, which can impact your overall performance. All great leaders, sitting in the middle chair, have developed a healthy mindset about themselves and those around them.

Sunny and I worked closely together to create new, healthy thought patterns. How? She learned to challenge her old assumptions objectively and strategically. For example, here is one of her thoughts we challenged:

Toxic Old Thought: *"I think I have to be perfect—there is no room to make any mistakes."*

Healthy New Thought: *"Stop focusing on perfection—it's impossible to achieve and will cause anxiety and stress for yourself and those around you. Instead, focus on excellence. Set realistic stretching goals, give it everything you have, and accept whatever your best is. Ask for feedback from your senior team and family at home. Listen carefully and use it as data to help you improve."*

Learning how to manage and control your attitude is one of the most important skills of all great leaders. In the book *The Power Of Story*, world-renowned performance psychologist Dr. Jim Loehr says, "According to two studies on brain function (Baumeister and Sommer; Bargh and Chartrand), 5 percent or less of the mind should be classified as the "conscious part"— controlled by self-regulatory, willful acts, while an astonishing 95 percent is nonconscious, automatic, instinctive."

Leaders take their power back when they stop to become more self-aware, start listening to the thoughts inside their mind that are like background music on repeat, and strategically challenge their thoughts with a new, truthful story. They become the authors of their life story, instead of reading their life story as it was given to them.

Dr. Loehr also says, "Every story we tell has some effect. Stories move the needle every time we tell them. Because of this powerful story effect, it's imperative that the story you tell be a constructive, and not destructive, one." How do you adopt the new story? He says, "By investing energy repeatedly and for as long as it takes until the new story becomes embedded, that is, becomes instinctual and irreversible."

When working with teams, the focus tends to be on learning communication skills and understanding group dynamics. However, when I coach individual leaders, emerging leaders, managers, senior leaders, and CEOs, much of my time is spent equipping them to develop this attitude skill—to cultivate a new, healthy mindset. It's equipping them to tell themselves truthful, kind statements, focusing on what they can control, and accepting what they cannot.

To help clients become more objective about their situation, I get them to write it down in second person—writing directed at "you."

This type of work feels like a battlefield, and it is. We charge toward deep-rooted, toxic thoughts that have plagued them for many years. It works, and it's so rewarding to see emotional chains that have pained leaders at every level of organizations, be broken and set them free.

Once clients identify their new, healthy thought, the next step is to read it at least twice daily. When we consistently train our brain to think differently, eventually our brain can adopt the new thought/attitude/mindset. How long does it take? That depends on the complexity of the toxic thought, how long you've been telling yourself that story, and how strategically and accurately you've challenged it.

One of my favorite books was written by psychiatrist Norman Doidge, author of *The Brain that Changes Itself,* who shares a metaphor developed by Harvard neurologist Alvaro Pascual-Leone about training your brain. Pascual-Leone states that the brain is more like plastic—and that it can change throughout one's life.

"The plastic brain is like a snowy hill in winter. Aspects of that hill—the slope, the rocks, the consistency of the snow—are, like our genes, a given. When we slide down on a sled, we can steer it and will end up at the bottom of the hill by following a path determined both by how we steer and the characteristics of the hill. Where exactly we will end up is hard to predict because there are so many factors in play. But what will definitely happen the second time you take the slope down is that you will more likely than not find yourself somewhere or another that is related to the path you took the first time. It won't be exactly that path, but it will be closer to that one than any other. And if you spend your afternoon sledding down, walking up, sledding down, at the end you will have some paths that have been used a lot, some that have been used very little…and there will be tracks that you have created, and it is very difficult now to get out of those tracks. And those tracks are not genetically determined anymore. The mental 'tracks' that get laid down can lead to habits, good or bad."

When we create new, healthy thoughts, it's like we are creating new tracks in our brain. It's empowering for many leaders to learn that their brain and attitude can be trained to think and act differently and, over time with conscious effort, to recognize the shift. This is great news.

HOW YOUR ATTITUDE AFFECTS
GOAL ATTAINMENT

How you feel about yourself shapes the goals you set and your likelihood of accomplishing them. Research published in the *International Journal of Environmental Research and Public Health*[28] indicates that people with low self-esteem—e.g., those in the right and left chairs—are more likely to self-sabotage, to reduce the chance that they will fail publicly. They expect unrealistic goals to be set for themselves and their team, which is exactly what Sunny had been doing. Researchers Locke and Lathan[29] found that "setting goals is linked with self-confidence, motivation, and autonomy." The ability to set goals reflects an individual's ability to see their future possibilities. Research from psychologist Gail Matthews[30] also found a strong connection between goal-setting and success. Individuals who are goal-oriented generally feel more positive about themselves; they believe they have the capacity to achieve.

Research has shown that by defining a realistic goal—something we want or want to achieve—and then taking the initiative to be successful, our brain rewires itself to link our ideal self-image with our identity. Interestingly, Matthews also found that when people write down their goals, they are 33 percent more successful than those who just formulate goals in their head.

When I first became interested in studying the power of attitudes, I read a lot of research, and witnessed it in my coaching practice, that when a person sets realistic goals that are meaningful to them, it is one of the best ways to build their confidence and sit in the middle chair. Why? Because when we set a goal and have the courage to step on the gas towards it, it builds self-efficacy—that's when a person believes they can impact how their life turns out. Self-efficacy is a super-power. For example, research in the *Academy of Management Journal*[31] found that self-efficacy is an important part of the relationship between goal-setting and higher performance. Research in the *Journal of Management*[32] confirms that self-efficacy impacts optimism and how people motivate themselves and persevere in overcoming obstacles.

Although we all have difficult circumstances in our lives that we cannot control (e.g., a critical boss, lack of career opportunities in the current company, racism, physical and learning disabilities, dysfunctional families, financial barriers) we can control putting our time and energy towards setting realistic goals in how to respond to those difficult circumstances. When we do that, we develop an empowered mindset (not a victim mindset). We learn that life is not happening to us—but we the author of our life story. That's why attitudes and goal-setting are so interconnected.

DEVELOPING LEADERSHIP SKILLS IN YOUNG PEOPLE

A couple of years ago, I was approached by researcher Dr. Naomi Thulien[33] from the MAP Centre for Urban Health Solutions at St. Michael's Hospital in Toronto, Canada, who wanted to know whether my leadership tools were applicable for all ages. If so, she wondered if I would I be willing to be part of a research study? Absolutely! Her area of focus was on helping young people (ages 18-26) transition away from homelessness. The research was named "*Identity Project*" and its purpose was to discover whether a program focused on developing identity capital (sense of purpose and control, self-efficacy and self-esteem) could improve the socioeconomic inclusion of young people who have experienced homelessness.

For this audience, I designed a customized six-week program using our existing tools from our SI: Leadership Coaching Program and got to work. The research that came out of that initiative was extremely positive, showing "statistically significant improvements and large effect size improvements in self-esteem" after the program. In only a short six-weeks, young people who had experienced challenges ranging from childhood abuse, to inadequate education, and few employment opportunities, and who had learned practical leadership tools, had increased hope, confidence, and were moving to the middle chair. The results were clear: Leadership development starts young, impacts everyone, is not fixed—but is rather teachable to anyone who is hungry to learn. This is great news!

What Effective Goal-Setting Looks Like

The Three Chairs are really about attitude and mindset. Attitude impacts everything, from your perspective to your communication, relationships, decision-making ability, stress management and goal-setting skills. If effective goal-setting is one of the best ways to move into the middle chair—what are the best practices I'm often asked? There are many tips, but here are **The 5S's of Effective Goal-Setting™**:

1: Stretching goals. Choosing target achievements that are realistic—meaning just beyond where you are now, rather than light years ahead—is critical for effectiveness. Be sure to write them down. Set a goal too low and you won't aspire to reach beyond that. Or set it so high that your inner skeptic tells you, "There's no way you'll be able to do that," and, as expected, you

MANY PEOPLE SET GOALS FOR THEMSELVES BUT THE PERCENTAGE WHO ACHIEVE THEM IS LOW. ACCORDING TO ONE *INC.* ARTICLE[34], ONLY EIGHT PERCENT OF PEOPLE ACHIEVE THEIR GOALS. THAT'S BECAUSE THERE IS A DIFFERENCE BETWEEN THINKING ABOUT A GOAL, WRITING IT DOWN AND TAKING INITIATIVE TOWARD THAT GOAL.

won't. Venture capitalist and author of *Measure What Matters*, John Doerr, says "For anyone striving for high performance in the workplace, goals are very necessary things." Doerr says the four superpowers are "focus, align, track, and stretch."

2: Striving for excellence, not perfection. Shooting for perfection is also unrealistic. It's unattainable. Instead, make your best effort your goal. Aim to perform at your highest level, and then be proud of yourself for what you're able to accomplish. Brené Brown writes in *The Gifts of Imperfection*, "Understanding the difference between healthy striving and perfectionism is critical to laying down the shield and picking up your life. Research shows that perfectionism hampers success. In fact, it's often the path to depression, anxiety, addiction, and life paralysis."

3: Seeking help. People who are confident in their abilities also know that they're not experts in everything. No one is. So, if there are tasks you need help with, be willing and able to ask for help from others. Being able to tap into others' expertise is the sign of a great leader. An article published in the *Harvard Business Review*[35] shared research that most people are happy to help; we just need to have the courage to ask. "When Vanessa Bohns, a professor at Cornell University and a leading researcher in this area, recently reviewed a group of experiments that she and her coauthors had done, she found that compliance—the rate at which people provided assistance to strangers who asked for it—was an average of 48 percent higher than the help seekers had expected. Clearly, people are much more likely to be helpful than we think they are," the *HBR* article reported.

4: Setting deadlines. There's a saying, "A goal is a dream with a deadline." Attaching a due date to a goal makes it much more attainable. With a deadline, you can work backward from that date to prepare a game plan for achievement. You can break down larger tasks into smaller chunks and chip away at them.

Without a deadline, your goal is just a wish, a hope—nothing more. For that reason, it's also unlikely to come to fruition.

5: Serenity and accepting the outcome. Focus on giving a stretch goal everything you can, strive for excellence, and accept whatever your best is—that is serenity. In fact, John Doerr[36] says, "If you're getting 100 percent of your OKRs [objectives and key results] done, that's not good. You probably weren't aggressive enough. A good grade at Intel or Google would be 70 percent." Similarly, goal-setting theory pioneers, as previously mentioned, Locke and Latham found scientific evidence to show that "the highest or most difficult goals produced the highest levels of effort and performance." It's important to accept the outcome because you can control your input (identifying a stretch goal and your effort towards it) but not the outcome (the result). Leaders in the middle chair focus on what they (and their teams) can control and accept what they cannot.

GREAT LEADERS ARE FLEXIBLE IN THEIR MINDSET AND GOAL-SETTING

Whether due to external or internal forces, flexibility and agility are crucial for success as a leader and as an organization. You may have heard of an agility quotient, or AQ, which is the ability to be flexible under pressure. It is the capacity to pivot when one approach isn't working or when market conditions change. The more agile a company, the faster it is able to pivot and shift gears with its goals.

Natalie Fratto[37], a vice president at Goldman Sachs, became interested in AQ when she was investing in a start-up and has since given a popular TED Talk. Fratto says "AQ is not just the capacity to absorb new information, but the ability to work out what is relevant, to unlearn obsolete knowledge, overcome challenges, and to make a conscious effort to change. AQ involves flexibility, curiosity, courage, resilience and problem-solving skills too."

Technology is changing the workforce. According to IBM[38], between 2019 and 2022, 120 million people, from the world's 12 largest economies, will need to be reskilled due to rising automation, making AQ even more important. As a leader, you need to be focused on the goals you've set but also be flexible, to account for changes that occur outside of your control that you then have to address or deal with. The speed with which you can shift your organization is a reflection of your AQ.

Fortunately, the ability to pivot can be learned. It's a lot like the thought process that skiers experience as they improve their skill, actually. When you're first learning to ski, you're taught to keep your eye focused on where you want to go. That determines the direction you're headed. But then you also need to keep your knees bent, flexible, to cushion any unexpected bumps in the terrain that you'll pass over. Great leaders in the middle chair carefully focus their time and energy on their attitude (CARDS™) and action (goal-setting). They focus on developing a healthy, empowering story, setting realistic goals (especially regarding difficult circumstances), staying focused yet flexible towards their goals.

Chapter 6 Action Steps: Apply the learning! Complete the exercise in *The Three Chairs: Workbook* & *Team Discussion Questions*. Go to www.dkleadership.org/thethreechairs for these bonus tools.

7

RELATIONSHIP SKILLS

"Let's invite one another in. Maybe then we can begin to fear less, to make fewer wrong assumptions, to let go of the biases and stereotypes that unnecessarily divide us. Maybe we can better embrace the ways we are the same. It's not about being perfect. It's not about where you get yourself in the end. There's power in allowing yourself to be known and heard, in owning your unique story, in using your authentic voice. And there's grace in being willing to know and hear others. This, for me, is how we become."

—Michelle Obama, former First Lady of
the U.S. and author of *Becoming*

As a leader, your relationship skills will determine your level of success. A great leader is capable of forming relationships and creating communities. That, in turn, helps create effective and more productive organizations. Researchers at Harvard[39] discovered that employees who felt cared for and supported in a platonic way experienced higher levels of satisfaction and teamwork. When their leader cultivated an emotional culture—one "where they felt free to express affection, tenderness, caring, and compassion for one another—employees were more satisfied with their jobs, committed to the organization, and accountable for their performance," according to the *Harvard Business Review*.

Author Simon Sinek says in his book *Start with Why: How Great Leaders Inspire Everyone to Take Action*, "Being the leader means you hold the highest rank, either by earning it, good fortune, or navigating internal politics. Leading, however, means that others willingly follow you—not because they have to, not because they are paid to, but because they want to." In order for people to want to follow you, it is essential that they feel valued, listened to, and understood. These are not suggestions; they are requirements for great relationships and for great leaders who sit in the middle chair.

UNDERSTANDING DIFFERENCES

There are many ways to build great relationships, and one of the key areas is by understanding and celebrating differences. Although there are many categories companies could focus on, those with the potential to yield the biggest results and the questions you need to answer for your team are:

- **Generational.** What do different generations value and how do they like to be managed?

- **Gender.** How do different genders often communicate?

- **Personality.** How do different personalities interpret information?

- **Cultural/Ethnicity.** How do different cultural groups communicate? How does systemic racism impact organizations?

Each of these differences could be its own chapter or book, so what follows is just a quick overview for you to start seeing life through another lens. Understanding and celebrating differences is a foundational skill of all great leaders who sit in the middle chair.

GENERATIONAL DIFFERENCES

My client Thomas is a brilliant, visionary leader. Charismatic and driven, he is adept at goal-setting and decision-making and, for that reason, things happen quickly inside his tech company. Many senior leaders there are like him—Gen Xers who prefer to work independently and don't require a lot of direction. To support the company's IT growth, Thomas has been hiring younger tech talent—typically millennials and Gen Zers. That shift created some issues which Thomas and the company hadn't faced before, mainly due to his old-school management style. One young employee felt unsupported at the company and ended up quitting. And that wasn't all. He felt so upset by the way he was treated that he took to social media to smear the company in retaliation. Thomas was blindsided by the attack.

Part of the problem was Thomas viewing the situation from his lens, not the lens of his employee. He couldn't empathize with the ex-employee and was perplexed by the feedback. When I started working with organizations 15 years ago (after focusing on millennials at my family coaching practice for 10 years), this topic was my speciality. I coached companies in how to equip managers and senior leaders to effectively manage the multi-generational workforce. It was immediately clear what Thomas had to do to fix this problem and increase the company's retention rate.

We started by having Thomas learn about the different generations, so that he could see the world through their eyes and experiences. Generations see the world differently and have different preferences for where, when, and how work gets done. That creates conflicts which get in the way of relationship-building. For example, baby boomers often value loyalty and hard work. So, leaving work before 5:00 pm may be perceived by them as slacking off. Likewise, switching jobs is seen by them as extremely disloyal. Research cited in *Business Insider*[40] from Public Affairs Research found that 40 percent of boomers stayed with their employers for at least 20 years, so many have difficulty comprehending how or why younger generations even consider leaving their current jobs.

Gen Xers typically value independence and work-life balance, according to King University[41], and millennials crave ongoing feedback, value entrepreneurship, and are more concerned with social responsibility. To that point, research by Deloitte[42] found that millennials "are generally more concerned with the social impact of a project, rather than the dollars and cents." They are also more likely to be future business owners. According to a *Forbes* article[43], Bentley University found that millennials are highly entrepreneurial: "almost two-thirds (67 percent) said their goal involves starting their own business." Thus, recognizing and respecting different generational values is a critical first step to forging positive relationships at work.

Understanding generational data can be helpful, but can also be problematic if we put people in boxes. People need to be given the opportunity to self-assess which generation they most connect to, rather than being told which they are most like. This is extremely important. For example, a first-generation immigrant may connect more to the boomer generation, while a millennial whose parents raised them counterculturally (i.e., if their parents didn't rescue them from failure), may connect more to the Gen X and boomer generations. Understanding generational trends can be useful, but what is most important is for managers to spend time getting to know each team member, what they value, and how they prefer to be managed. Only then can one know how they work best and what kind of support they need or prefer.

I helped Thomas understand that most millennials want to do a great job for their manager and the best way for them to improve is to hear ongoing feedback. It's a very logical approach. As Thomas began to understand this different perspective, his posture changed, "Okay, Karyn, you have a good point. I need you to talk to my senior team so that they can understand this, because they're all like me." That is another common problem—we tend to hire people just like us, so there is often insufficient understanding of other generations than our own.

GENDER DIFFERENCES

What is the gender diversity of your senior leadership team? This is a critical question, because companies need diversity to perform at their best. Great leaders, sitting in the middle chair, are humble—they admit they don't know everything, which is why they prioritize diversity at all levels within their organization. They surround themselves with others from whom they can learn. Diversity is critical for business success. There is substantial research showing a correlation between diversity and business performance. An article from the World Economic Forum[44] reported that diversity brings "many advantages to an organization: increased profitability and creativity, stronger governance, and better problem-solving abilities ... A Boston Consulting Group study[45] found that companies with more diverse management teams have 19 percent higher revenues due to innovation."

Gender is a complex topic that must be approached with sensitivity. Today we know that gender is more fluid than people first thought, and that while some people identify as male, and some as female, others identify as gender-neutral or as some other non-binary gender variant. So how best to approach this? Great leaders sitting in the middle chair will empathetically listen to understand each person's unique story, even though they may not understand or relate to it, and aim to create an inclusive workplace. That may include revising application forms, hiring guidelines, or promotion rubrics. For example, *USA Today*[47] reported, "In 2014, the University of Vermont became the first school to allow students to select their preferred pronouns, like xe or zir, in a campus-wide database. Harvard University, the

University of California system, and the University of Tennessee, among others, have since followed suit."

Although some gender differences are myths—e.g., that women talk more than men, which was refuted by research at the University of Arizona[48] which found that *both* men and women say approximately 16,000 words a day—others are valid. *Forbes*[49] reported that women use five tones when speaking, giving them more emotional range when communicating, while men only use three, which can make them seem more monotone and unaffected. Research conducted in United States, Canada, and Europe by Dr. Carol Kinsey Gorman, and published in the same article, also found that men may be more direct in their communication style and women more empathetic. Men tend to take up more physical space when communicating, while women often reduce their space. On the other hand, women make more eye contact and provide more facial expressions when communicating than men. These differences affect how men and women are perceived at work and can impede or foster their ability to build relationships.

The struggle for gender equity in the workplace (and elsewhere) has come a long way since "women's lib" burst on the scene in the 1960s, but still has a long way to go. Today's business leaders can facilitate that goal by proactively understanding and honoring gender differences.

PERSONALITY DIFFERENCES

Another big impediment to relationship-building is personality differences—individual traits and behaviors that shape how we respond to various situations. Great leaders take the time to get to know individuals and seek to understand their backstory, or why they act the way they do. There are many tools and assessments that can be used to help teams understand themselves and each other.

Although understanding personality differences may seem obvious, those differences can wreak havoc on relationships. I experienced this firsthand 15 years ago, when I started expanding the focus of our work from family systems to organizations. I met with three senior leaders and four CEOs to discuss a national partnership campaign that they were kicking off. I was the only woman sitting at the table, so I was outnumbered from the get-go. In front of the group, one CEO said abruptly, "Karyn, if you want to continue to work with corporations, you'd better learn how to spell people's names correctly." Instantly I felt embarrassed and irritated that he would publicly give constructive feedback. When I later shared the story with my husband and business partner, he interpreted the situation differently and knowing the CEO, said in a kind yet matter-of-fact way, "Karyn, he was just trying to be helpful."

> SOME OF THE MOST POPULAR SELF-ASSESSMENT TOOLS ARE: STRENGTHSFINDER, DISC ASSESSMENT, MYERS-BRIGGS TYPE INDICATOR, PREDICTIVE INDEX, KOLBE A INDEX, ENNEAGRAM, THE BIRKMAN METHOD, AND EQ-I 2.0. THERE IS NO RIGHT OR WRONG ANSWER HERE. CHOOSE THE TOOL THAT COMES CLOSEST TO TELLING YOU WHAT YOU WANT TO LEARN ABOUT YOURSELF AND/OR YOUR EMPLOYEES.

The truth was—I did spell a person's name incorrectly. It was a good learning opportunity, reminding me of the importance of taking my time to double-check my work. As a feeler, I needed to remember not to personalize the feedback (a common issue for feelers). Conversely, thinkers often have to learn to communicate with more empathy to get buy-in from their teams, which is a common complaint *they* hear. The reality is, we need both approaches. As our business has significantly grown, and most of our clients are CEOs and senior leadership teams, I take a solution-oriented, direct-but-kind approach with my high-powered clients, which they value, and which is highly effective for all personalities.

Cultural Differences and Systemic Racism

Being raised in families with different traditions can also affect how people communicate at work. Whereas Japanese culture values indirect communication, that approach can be misunderstood by Americans as tacit approval. Similarly, the directness that some Scandinavian cultures express can be perceived as rude by employees in North America. There is no right or wrong, only an opportunity to recognize that some differences result from culture.

Harvard research states that we all have unconscious bias. To help us all recognize and understand the bias we *all* have, a team there developed a free Unconscious Bias Test[50], which is designed for people to consciously change their mindset in order to drive positive change.

One important type of bias that happens in the workplace is around race, frequently due to systemic racism. As I was writing this book in May 2020, George Floyd was brutally killed and the anti-Black racism movement exploded. Many of us, and especially those of us who are White, feel uncomfortable discussing racism, so we usually don't. And yet, if we—meaning *all* of us—White, Black, Indigenous, and People of Color (POC), want to sit in the middle chair, it is essential that we lean in to understand the complexities of racism, to listen and learn from each other.

Racism is fueled by people who sit in the right and left chairs, who consciously or unconsciously believe that their race is superior. Anti-racist activist Peggy McIntosh[51] says, "I was taught to see racism only in individual acts of meanness, not in invisible systems conferring dominance on my group." This means a leader could be simultaneously sitting in the middle chair—i.e., consciously anti-racist, as expressed in the common statement, "I'm not racist"—and sitting in the right or left chair, unconsciously biased by discriminating against or not speaking up for non-White people. Research confirms this. An article published by the *Harvard Business School*[52] states that research from the University of Toronto discovered that "25 percent of black candidates received call-backs from their whitened résumés, while only 10 percent got calls when they left ethnic details intact."

There are many layers to racism, but let's focus on "White privilege," because it's often misunderstood, impacts racial conditioning, and adversely affects the workforce. McIntosh, in her groundbreaking essay, "White Privilege: Unpacking the Invisible Knapsack," says White privilege "doesn't mean that you are being labeled as someone who is actively prejudiced toward non-White people. Instead, it is making the point that as a White person, you receive benefits from being the dominant ethnicity in society." She asks dozens of questions, but ask yourself if you agree or disagree with these two statements, to get a sense of how privileged you are (assuming you are White):

- "I can go home from most meetings of organizations I belong to feeling somewhat tied in, rather than isolated, out-of-place, outnumbered, unheard, held at a distance, or feared."

- "I can go shopping alone most of the time, pretty well assured that I will not be followed or harassed."

The impact of racial conditioning is predictable. Many White people unconsciously or consciously learn: "I belong. I matter. I'm safe. I'm deserving." Meanwhile, many Black or POC unconsciously or consciously learn: "I don't belong. I don't matter. My voice is not important. I'm not safe. I'm inferior." Think now about how this racial conditioning impacts The Three Chairs—where people sit and how they treat others in hiring, promotions, and team dynamics, consciously and unconsciously.

So what can we do for ourselves and our teams? If you are White, here are a few suggestions (we are only scratching the surface on this) for actions you can take today. If you are Black or a Person Of Color, you might consider sharing this with your colleagues at work:

1: Talk Openly About Racism and White Privilege
Silence perpetuates racism (left chair)! We need to lean into this uncomfortable topic and speak out when we see racism happen (middle chair).

2: Seek more Diversity
How much diversity do you have in your organization across all levels of leadership, from emerging to manager to senior leader? Does it mirror your community's ethnicity? Avoid an attitude of tokenism here; the goal is not to check off the box that says "We have X percent Black colleagues," but rather that you value diversity and want everyone's voices in your board-room and at all levels in your company.

3: Change the Racism Question
If you really want to discuss racial equity with your teams at work, don't discuss racism from a binary yes or no ("Are you racist?") lens. Instead shift to "how." *How* are we allowing racism to function in our business? Within our teams? What is the ethnic makeup of our leadership team?

4: Be Committed to Racial Equity
Author Ibram X. Kendi says, "the heartbeat of racism is denial," so it's critical that we see this as a lifelong journey and commit to ongoing learning. Here are a couple of great books on the topic: *How to Be An Antiracist,* by Ibram X. Kendi, and *White Fragility: Why It's So Hard For White People To Talk About Racism,* by Dr. Robin DiAngelo.

5: Focus on White Responsibility, Not White Guilt
We cannot control the color of our skin, but we can control how we respond today. Shift your focus from guilt (which is usually driven by thoughts such as "I should...") to responsibility. Ask yourself, "How can I use my White privilege to empower and create more opportunities for Blacks and POC, because I want to, not because I have to."

In summary, great leaders who sit in the middle chair prioritize building great relationships (CA**R**DS™). They realize that there are many differences among people—generational, personality, gender, cultural and racial, et al. But instead of judging, blaming, and excluding, great leaders lean in to understand them, discover how they are similar, celebrate differences, and listen to others' needs, so they can effectively lead them by building strong relationships.

Chapter 7 Action Steps: Apply the learning! Complete the exercise in *The Three Chairs: Workbook* & *Team Discussion Questions.* Go to www.dkleadership.org/thethreechairs for these bonus tools.

8

DECISION-MAKING, TIME MANAGEMENT, AND SELF-DISCIPLINE SKILLS

"Being overwhelmed is often as unproductive as
doing nothing, and is far more unpleasant. Being
selective—doing less—is the path of the productive.
Focus on the important few and ignore the rest."

—Timothy Ferriss, author of *The 4-Hour Workweek*

Many times I have been asked by senior managers to coach one of their employees, usually to prepare them for a promotion or more senior leadership role. But when Abigail pulled me aside to talk about her boss, Kerri—a senior manager in human resources at a fast-growing accounting firm, that was a first. Abigail was Kerri's assistant, and told me she was concerned because Kerri was running herself ragged, working around the clock now that her kids were out of the house, which was negatively impacting her performance and reputation. Other people were noticing that Kerri was *constantly* working, and that wasn't a good thing.

Kerri had always been a top performer, but recently she'd been slipping—she wasn't as "together" as she once had been.

The company had grown significantly in two years and, as a result, the workloads were much heavier. However, Kerri hadn't adjusted her new responsibilities with high performance habits. She hadn't begun to use daily routines, self-discipline boundaries, priorities, and delegation as tactics to match her increased workload. And that wasn't all. She also wasn't as joyful to be around at work. Her whole team was worried about her, Abigail confided. They wanted her to get help to avoid the burnout that was clearly coming. They wanted her to be able to sit in the middle chair again—to be a great leader.

THE POWER OF A DAILY ROUTINE

We started by looking at Kerri's schedule. Almost every leadership expert will talk about this simple habit—developing an inspiring and practical daily routine is required for high performance.

Looking at Kerri's schedule, it was structured to include working from the time she woke up to the time she went to bed. Although this approach is similar to many leaders, it had to change. Focusing solely on work 24/7 is not sustainable. Kerri needed to build in breaks, so we revamped her whole schedule to make time for non-work activities. "What one activity outside of work do you find highly energizing?" I asked her. Turns out, Kerri is a marathon runner. That led to arranging her schedule so that she started each day with a morning run. She could start her day on a high. Next, we looked at her daily work schedule, which was crammed full of tasks and meetings. I encouraged her to focus on her most important priorities first, while she had the most energy, and then her afternoons would be open for team meetings. I taught her the

> "THE MOST SUCCESSFUL PEOPLE ALL HAVE CERTAIN HABITS IN THEIR DAILY ROUTINES. 1. PLAN YOUR DAY THE NIGHT BEFORE 2. SET PRIORITIES ON YOUR TO-DO LIST BEFORE YOU START THE DAY 3. COMPLETE THE MOST IMPORTANT DAILY TASK FIRST." —BRIAN TRACY

adage of Parkinson's Law, which states that tasks expand to fill the time allotted. If you have an hour to write a memo, it's very likely it will take you a full hour to complete it, even if, when focused, you could have completed it in 15 minutes.

This is why workers at all levels of an organization often put off work until later. They procrastinate. If they don't get that research done by 5:00 pm today they'll just do it that evening at home, they tell themselves. Creating high performance boundaries in the morning for priorities inspired Kerri to get her priorities done during that window of time. Finally, we talked about shutting off her computer in the evening. Staying connected to work was exhausting and was causing her team stress, thinking they had to be available to her day and night. It was a downward spiral. Kerri's goal was to be a great leader, but her poor time-management and self-discipline was making that impossible with the increased workload from the company's growth. Although this isn't unusual in fast-growing organizations, it's important to make changes quickly for sustained high performance and to avoid burnout.

> BOUNDARIES ARE CRITICAL FOR PROTECTING YOURSELF AND AVOIDING BURNOUT. IMAGINE THAT YOU'RE A CANDLE. IF I PUT YOU BY AN OPEN WINDOW, THE DRAFT WILL BLOW YOU OUT—THERE'S TOO MUCH AIR COMING THROUGH AT ONCE. BUT IF I PUT A PIECE OF GLASS IN FRONT OF YOU, TO PROTECT YOUR FLAME, YOU WILL CONTINUE TO BURN BRIGHTLY. THAT'S HOW BOUNDARIES WORK: HEALTHY BOUNDARIES PROTECT YOUR EMOTIONAL, MENTAL, PHYSICAL WELL-BEING AND ENERGY.

WORK WITH YOUR CIRCADIAN RHYTHM

Once clients have a first draft of their new high-performance daily routine, they begin to test drive it. What works, what doesn't? Ask yourself the same kinds of questions. Increase your self-awareness so you can tweak your daily routine to maximize performance.

One likely reason for those energy ups and downs is your circadian rhythm. An article in *Harvard Business Review*[53] states, "Humans have a well-defined internal clock that shapes our energy levels throughout the day: our circadian process, which is often referred to as a circadian rhythm because it tends to be very regular... This natural—and hardwired—ebb and flow in our ability to feel alert or sleepy has important implications for you and your employees. Although managers expect their employees to be at their best at all hours of the workday, it's an unrealistic expectation... Managers who want to maximize their employees' performance should consider this circadian rhythm when setting assignments, deadlines, and expectations."

Tackle your top priorities first. Putting those types of activities off until later tends to increase your anxiety, because of the looming deadline. Daniel Pink, author of, *When: The Scientific Secrets of Perfect Timing,* says, "Decisions and negotiations should be conducted earlier in the day."

THE SELF-DISCIPLINE, DECISION-MAKING AND TIME-MANAGEMENT LINK

When I coach clients to increase their productivity and reduce their stress, I often start by helping them design an inspiring-yet-practical high-performance daily routine. That becomes the structure—the healthy boundaries to optimize their performance. Next, we work on understanding and developing the self-discipline muscle to execute the plan. Many people can design their routine, but do they have the discipline to follow it? That often becomes the challenge. This was one of Kerri's roadblocks. Her internal conflict was between her head and her heart, her mindset and her feelings. I explained to her that your head focuses on the big-picture—your values, goals, and, ultimately, what is the best for you. It is strategic. Your heart focuses on feeling good and avoiding pain right now. It focuses on the present moment. Our head and heart will each have its own opinion about every decision we make in life—career, exercise, time-management, finance, spouses, et al. Decisions are a lot simpler if our head and heart are aligned—for example, if we get a promotion that is our dream job with increased pay, which pleases our head, and it's work we feel passionate about, which pleases our heart. But what happens if our head and heart are not aligned? If we want to lose weight, our head tells us, but this requires regular exercise and eating healthy, which makes us feel unmotivated in the moment, according to our heart. Lead with your head, your heart will catch up—essentially that's what self-discipline is.

I dug deeper with Kerri to understand her decision-making process as it related to her time-management and self-discipline. I asked her:

- What's your *head* telling you? She said, "I want to do a great job and take care of my teams."

- What is your *heart* telling you? She said, "I feel afraid, uncomfortable, guilty."

When I asked her *why* she felt those feelings, she answered, "I feel afraid because I don't want people to think I'm not a high-performer. Our firm has grown significantly in the last couple of years and I want to show the senior team that I'm highly capable. I feel uncomfortable saying no—it's just easier for me to do things myself. I feel guilty taking time off, even to take care of myself," Kerri told me. She was leading with her heart. To avoid feeling uncomfortable, she was taking on more work, not delegating, not asking for help, not saying "no." In the moment it felt better to avoid pain, but in the big picture, that decision seriously backfired, because now she felt exhausted and close to burnout. That's the price tag when we are not self-disciplined.

I encouraged Kerri to flip the scenario. If she led with her head, what would it say? She told me: "Do what is best, not what is easy and comfortable. Prioritize your most important tasks. Say 'no.' Delegate to your team; they want more work. Take care of yourself—you have only one health. Create a great routine. Set boundaries. Teach others your optimal high-performance schedule." I then asked her, how would your heart feel as you implement this plan? "Scared, uncomfortable," she replied. How would you feel *after* you've prioritized, delegated, and set boundaries? "Energized, empowered, positive, productive." Yes, exactly!

When we lead with our head, our heart catches up. Ask anyone who has tried to lose weight, save money, start a new career, or apply for a promotion. Each goal is scary and uncomfortable. But *after* they've lost weight and fit in their old jeans, saved money and bought their first house, finished their MBA, and gotten the promotion, how do they feel? Confident, motivated, empowered, energized, and happy! Great leaders, sitting in the middle chair are highly self-disciplined.

That's why self-discipline is not only linked to more productivity, but also happiness. Research published in the *Journal of Personality*[54] found a strong connection between higher levels of self-control and life satisfaction. According to Wilhelm Hofmann and his team of researchers at the University of Chicago[55], "Among humankind's most valuable assets is self-control" which they describe as "the ability to override or change one's inner responses."

This is a topic that is well researched and accepted by industry leaders. Even the Dalai Lama XIV says in his book *The Art of Happiness,* "A disciplined mind leads to happiness, and an undisciplined mind leads to suffering." The great news is that self-discipline is like a muscle that we can train.

COUNTERCULTURAL MESSAGES

Be aware that this leadership principle is the exact opposite of what our culture often teaches. Watch children's movies, listen to lyrics in music, see it in inspirational quotes, and a common line you will hear is "follow your heart," which is terrible advice when it comes to leadership development. Culturally, we have not properly educated children and adults about emotion management, feelings, and how it relates to decision-making and self-discipline. If you follow your heart, which wants to feel good and avoid pain *now*, this means you will do what is easy, comfortable, and familiar. Here are examples of decisions dictated by feelings that I heard my clients say that guided their poor decisions and which, afterwards, they all regretted:

- *I felt "unmotivated," so therefore I decided to procrastinate finishing a major contract.*

- *I felt "embarrassed," so I didn't tell my boss that I made a mistake and, instead, covered it up.*

- *I felt "uncomfortable and scared" to put my name forward for a promotion, so I didn't.*

They all knew what they wanted to do—what their head was telling them to do, but their feelings—their heart—ultimately made the decision for them. If you want to be a great leader, sitting in the middle chair, you need to listen to your heart, yet lead with your head. That is self-discipline.

Similarly, renowned keynote speaker, CNN legal and social commentator, and author Mel Robbins writes in *The 5 Second Rule: Transform Your Life, Work, and Confidence with Everyday Courage*, "You aren't battling your ability to stick to a diet, execute a business plan, repair a broken marriage and rebuild your life, hit your goals, or win over a bad manager—you are battling your feelings about doing it. You are more than capable of doing the work to change anything for the better, despite how you feel. Feelings are merely suggestions, ones you can ignore. To change you must do the same, you must ignore how you feel, and just do it anyway."

HIGH PERFORMER HABITS—FOCUS ON YOUR TOP THREE PRIORITIES

Prioritizing is a must for great leaders sitting in the middle chair. It's a skill that can help pull the critical tasks to the fore and push the less essential to the back. But if you have too many high priority tasks, you really just have a super long list. Determine which three of your responsibilities are the most critical. Those are your top priorities (for now).

This is likely why Google uses objectives and key results (OKRs)[56], which are like key performance indicators (KPI), to help their employees challenge themselves and make better decisions. OKRs were introduced by an early Google investor, John Doerr, who explained that everyone in the organization should answer 1) where am I headed and 2) how will I pace myself to recognize my progress? There are annual and quarterly OKRs that are shared company-wide, to get everyone on the same page. OKRs are measured on a scale of 0 to 100. Low scores suggest the OKR needs to be recalibrated, while high scores suggest the OKR wasn't challenging enough. Google recognized the importance of company-wide alignment on goal-setting, measurement of progress, and recalibration each quarter.

HIGH PERFORMANCE HABITS— START WITH YOUR LENS™

Many executives value practical decision-making tools. Because many clients get stuck and feel overwhelmed on their priorities, I created a tool called LENS™. This tool helps identify what to do first. It consists of the following four easy steps:

L = List everything you need to do to complete a task on your to-do list.

E = Estimate how long each step will take.

N = Number each step, in order, that will be necessary to complete the work.

S = Schedule when to complete each step, starting with the first.

When you work through the LENS™ process, you reduce the stress of wondering how to start.

Breaking each priority down into smaller chunks makes anything less overwhelming and more manageable, creating energy for action. It's so simple that even my kids started using LENS™ as early as fourth grade.

HIGH PERFORMANCE HABITS— DELEGATION IS A LEADERSHIP TACTIC

Another important habit of great leaders to drive productivity is to delegate to other professionals. An article in the *Globe and Mail*[7] cited research from London Business School professor John Hunt, who found that only "30 percent of managers think they can delegate well, and of those, only one in three is considered a good delegator by his or her subordinates."

Sometimes the benefits of delegating can be hard to see, however, especially for high performers.

My client Kellen was certainly a superstar, and a recently promoted manager. He was also a perfectionist who had a hard time handing off work to others. His team was actually craving the opportunity to do more for him, especially his millennial team members, who told me they were getting "bored." They wanted more challenges; they wanted to contribute. But Kellen just wouldn't let them. One of the first things I helped him see was that he needed to start delegating to his team. Yes, it was hard, but part of being a great leader, sitting in the middle chair, requires that you trust and delegate, give regular ongoing feedback, and be accessible when team members have questions. Although he was tentative at first about handing off work, he quickly saw the benefits. Kellen's workload became manageable, his team was happy to have more challenging work, they were much more engaged, and thus were more likely to stay.

Decision-making, time management, prioritization and self-discipline are all related. It may seem easier to do the work yourself, but long-term, that's not an effective leadership strategy. Great leaders, sitting in the middle chair, focus on developing this CARD**S**™ skill by structuring their time for high performance, developing their self-discipline muscle (i.e., leading with their head and feeling the benefits after), focusing on their three priorities using LENS™ to take action, and delegating to their team in order to drive high productivity.

Chapter 8 Action Steps: Apply the learning! Complete the exercise in *The Three Chairs: Workbook* & *Team Discussion Questions.* Go to www.dkleadership.org/thethreechairs for these bonus tools.

9

STRESS, ANXIETY, AND EMOTION MANAGEMENT SKILLS

"We can choose courage or we can choose comfort,
but we can't have both. Not at the same time."

—Brené Brown, author of *Rising Strong*

When I began working with my client Hudson, CEO of a successful second-generation family business, he was stressed about several aspects of his life. In addition to grappling with the decision of what to do with his family's company—continue running it, sell it, or shut it down—he had grown distant from his wife and son. They were no longer connecting, which was a source of disappointment that only heightened his stress. Employees had commented that he was short-tempered in his communication with them. He was also procrastinating more, which made his workload back up and become almost insurmountable. He was overwhelmed. Without any close relationships to refuel him and lower his stress and anxiety, he turned to me for help. We started by trying to identify what, specifically, was causing him stress. Although we can't directly control our feelings, like turning a light switch on or off, we can change them indirectly by changing our attitude and actions. But the truth is that his stress was not the problem, because feelings never are. However, it was a clue to another problem. "Your feelings are your friend," I told him, "not the enemy. They are there to tell you something. We need to lean in and figure this out."

DIFFERENTIATING EMOTIONS AND FEELINGS

How are emotions different from feelings? Many people use the words interchangeably, and while they are highly related, they are different. Antonio Damasio, professor of neuroscience at the University of California[58] explains it like this: "Feelings are mental experiences of body states, which arise as the brain interprets emotions, themselves physical states arising from the body's responses to external stimuli." Meaning, events will happen in our life and we will experience emotions that manifest as physical sensations, such as our heart racing, stomach churning or facial expressions. How we interpret those events are mental, including thoughts, attitudes, mindset, and the internal story we tell ourselves, which in turn drive our feelings and then our performance. It's a domino effect, which is all part of understanding emotion management, which is a critical skill for great leaders who sit in the middle chair.

So how to get started? One of the first steps for all leaders is to stop and identify their feelings. In fact, research from UCLA[59] found that by simply naming a troubling feeling "you can calm yourself and your brain down." After having difficulty at first, Hudson was eventually able to name his feelings. He acknowledged that he felt uncertainty and anxiety about the business. He felt pressured to run it, and was worried about failing his family's legacy. He was also worried about his personal relationships with his wife and son. Once we uncovered the source of his feelings, step one, we created a strategic plan to address the situations.

START WITH AN EASY WIN

Start by addressing the easiest problem first, so that you can quickly see progress. Hudson started with his 20-year-old son. The two men are very different and his son was making choices that Hudson didn't understand, although he wanted to. Hudson also worried that his son might be feeling pressured to follow his father into the business. His son was sensitive and somewhat closed off, so we focused on learning how to get his son to open up. Simple-but-effective approaches include:

- Choosing a good time to talk one-on-one, when you are both relaxed and won't be interrupted.

- Evenings and late at night tend to work best for young people.

- Talk "sideways" and avoid eye contact, which helps to reduce anxiety when discussing tricky topics with young people.

- Focus on having a discussion involving two-way communication, rather than an interrogation and lecture; use lines like "I'm curious."

Hudson chose courage over comfort, in Brené Brown's words, and they made great progress. Hudson learned through a few late-night conversations that his son didn't want to run the business. Although Hudson was disappointed, he understood. He didn't have to guess any more about his son's level of interest in the business, and now Hudson could make decisions about what *he* wanted to do with the business.

Hudson also chose "courage over comfort" with his wife. He learned that she felt caught in the middle between her husband and son. She, too, was highly sensitive, so she felt the tension between them. Now that Hudson's communication was calmer with their son, she felt better about their dynamic.

Hudson then shifted his attention to the family business. Many leaders find understanding feelings more complicated and illogical than they would like, which causes more anxiety. The solution to reducing that anxiety is education. When leaders understand how feelings logically work, they are empowered to take action. Ask yourself three key questions:

1. Thoughts: What are my thoughts?

2. Feelings: What are my feelings (from those thoughts)?

3. Actions: How do my feelings impact my performance, including my communication, motivation, decision-making, body language, sleep, eating, or exercise?

Recognizing and understanding the linkage—the domino effect among these three parts—is foundational to mastering emotion-management skills.

DIFFERENTIATING THOUGHTS AND FEELINGS

What is the difference between a thought and a feeling? Surprisingly, 90 percent of people I ask, who are extremely accomplished and highly educated, do not successfully answer this question. This is a big problem, because great leaders who sit in the middle chair need to understand this in order to be effective communicators.

This is actually a great EQ question. As psychologist Daniel Goleman put it in a TED Talk[60] called "Why Aren't We More Compassionate?," "There is zero correlation between IQ and emotional empathy ... they're controlled by different parts of the brain." That's why people can have three PhDs and still not understand feelings and emotion management.

Here is a quick cheat sheet to help you differentiate between thoughts and feelings:

Thoughts	Feelings
Many words.	One word. *(For example: Anxious, stressed, overwhelmed.)*
Often start with "I think ...."	Often start with "I feel..." We have hundreds of feelings.
Logical or illogical.	Always logical. *(Hint. The thought that's driving it may be illogical but feelings are logical.)*
Can control.	Can't directly control. *(Hint. But you can indirectly change it if you change your thoughts and actions.)*
You can respectfully challenge, debate a person's thought.	You should never challenge a person's feeling because they can't directly control it. *(Hint: Avoid statements like "You shouldn't feel....")*

While experts differ on how many feelings we have, with some saying we have thousands, many believe that feelings can be grouped into clusters and are highly connected. Research from the University of California at Berkeley[61] identified "27 distinct categories."

Here's a quick test: Is this sentence a thought or feeling?

"I feel as though you did a terrible job on this project. Don't challenge me, because that's how I feel."

Answer: It's actually a thought. Why? Because there is no feeling word in that sentence. Just because a person uses the word "feel" in a sentence doesn't mean it's a feeling. Why is this a problem? Because the receiver will feel trapped, that they can't challenge it. Remember, you can challenge thoughts, perspectives, or opinions—but never challenge feelings. The correct syntax would be:

"I feel frustrated (feeling) because I think you did a terrible job on this project (thought)."

Great leaders who sit in the middle chair can empathize with someone's feelings and respectfully challenge their thinking. Learning how to differentiate between thoughts and feelings is critical in managing your own emotions and effectively communicating with others.

TAKING THE FEELING OUT OF THE DECISION

Hudson's next task was to dial in, specifically, what he was feeling about the family business and what thoughts were driving it. Once he had that data, he would be able to make a clear decision. This is how emotion management impacts all other parts of leadership—communication, our relationship with others, our decision-making, and performance. What felt like a big knot of feelings in his stomach, Hudson was able to untangle and identify:

- "I feel overwhelmed, burdened, anxiety (feelings) because I think the family's legacy is on my shoulders and I don't know what is going to happen (thought)."

- "I feel stress (feeling) because I don't know if I really want to keep the company (thought)."

It had become a never-ending circle of anxiety and stress. Hudson needed to sort out his relationship to his job and the family's company. To do that, he needed to ask himself:

- Is this really what I want? Does this business align with my values?

- Would I prefer to sell the company or hire someone else to run it?

- Do we need the finances?

By separating what he "should" do from what he "wanted" to do, looking at the situation more objectively, Hudson recognized what he knew all along: He didn't want to be there. That's why he was procrastinating, not being fully present. His son also didn't want to run it. Hudson decided to sell the business and use the revenue to start a new venture in real estate.

With decision-making, it's important to listen to your heart—which may be feeling stress, anxiety, and burden—to understand the thoughts as data. You can then be objective and lead with your head, which is guided by your values and goals. When Hudson did this, he felt relief almost immediately.

CURBING ANXIETY AND BUILDING RESILIENCE

Anxiety has become epidemic in America. An article in *Psychology Today*[62] on anxiety states, "The Gallup World Emotions Report shows a rise in stress and worry... Greece and the U.S. lead the world in adult stress levels at fifty-nine and fifty-five percent respectively ... This means that despite a growing American economy, adults in the U.S. are more worried, stressed, and angry." And these rates were on the rise even before COVID-19.

Why the increase? There are many theories—perfectionism, uncertainty about the future, one's boss, a lot of change, what we see in the news, or social media. There is one common element, though, with every kind of anxiety: it focuses on what we cannot control. That's the problem.

When I started coaching millennials more than 20 years ago, I started seeing anxiety spike among my clients. Let me say, if you are experiencing any stress, anxiety, depression or other unpleasant feelings, I strongly recommend that you see your family physician to assess the physical side, and then ask them to recommend a great counselor or solution-oriented therapist to help you learn how to manage the emotional part. We need support on both sides—physical and emotional—because the two are highly interconnected.

The physicians I worked with focused on the physical side, treating conditions such as heart racing, sleeping, difficult breathing, while I focused on teaching practical emotion management tools for clients to learn how to manage anxiety instead of anxiety managing them. Clients motivated to put the tools into action saw significant results. So when we expanded our work with organizations, the topic of anxiety was popular with leaders who wanted to learn.

Managing anxiety is important for success. When anxiety is high, it can interfere with high performance, creating such blockages as difficulty concentrating, poor communication, procrastinating, perfection and/or burn out. The great news is, it's the mindset that often drives the anxiety and that's where you need to put your focus.

An article in *Forbes*[63], citing research from the *Journal of Individual Differences*, notes that "Those who viewed stressful events as challenges—rather than threats—gained energy from their anxiety. The boost in energy motivated them and improved their performance. The researchers discovered individuals performed best when they acknowledged their anxiety—as opposed to suppressing it."

What's really important is how we interpret events and the stories we tell ourselves. This speaks to our resilience. People who sit in the middle chair are not void of problems or stressors; rather, it's their mindset towards them that is different. An article in *The Washington Post*[64] shares a psychologist's science-based tips for emotional resilience during the coronavirus crisis, reporting, "Studies show that people who go through very difficult life experiences can emerge from them with a stronger sense of psychological resilience[65]." Here are some simple tips to help you understand anxiety and action steps to make progress:

- While stress tends to focus on time management (e.g., "I feel stressed because I don't have enough time to complete this project"), anxiety tends to focus on future events (e.g., "I feel anxious because what if _____").

- Facing your anxiety, and creating a realistic action plan to deal with it, will shrink anxiety. Avoiding it will make it grow bigger.

- Anxiety is a feeling that is neither good nor bad. It is there to help you not harm yourself. It has a message for you, so pay attention!

- Listen to the feeling, but more importantly: dig in and understand the thought that's driving it.

- No one else can make you feel anxious. Other people may perform hurtful, insensitive, and malicious actions, but how you interpret those events (thoughts) and how you respond (actions), will determine how you feel. You have full control of your attitude and actions. Put 100 percent of your energy and focus there.

- Many thoughts that are causing anxiety are toxic, especially perfectionism (e.g., "I think I have to be perfect"). The toxic thoughts are the problem, not the anxiety. Change the toxic thought to be truthful and kind, focusing on what you can control and accepting what you cannot control. Write out your new, healthy thoughts. If you get stuck, ask someone whom you trust, who is sitting in the middle chair, how they would replace the thought.

- Often people who sit in the right and left chairs set their goals too high (perfectionism), or too low (avoiding it), and will often struggle with anxiety. Focus carefully on setting realistic goals and strive for excellence.

Bestselling author Michael Hyatt of *Platform: Get Noticed in a Noisy World,* wisely says, "Perfectionism is the mother of procrastination." Great leaders, who sit in the middle chair, are extremely careful of the thoughts they tell themselves. They lovingly and strategically put their focus on what they can control and accept what they cannot control.

STRESS AND WHY REFUELING IS CRITICAL

The impact of a leadership role on stress is conflicting. Some studies report that the more senior your title, the higher your stress levels, presumably because of the responsibility you feel to your community—employees, vendors, customers, investors, and family. However, other research from the *Proceedings from the National Academy of Sciences*[66] found that the higher you rise in the management hierarchy, the lower your stress level, because you have more control over your situation and decisions. Regardless of whether you feel more or less stress as a leader, the truth remains that great leaders who sit in the middle chair manage their stress by focusing on these two priorities:

(1) Effective time-management, few priorities and delegation

(2) Effective refueling (prioritizing self-care)

Celine is the manager of a healthcare organization which, during the global pandemic, has been on the front lines of helping patients.

> "IF YOU HAVE TOO MANY TOP PRIORITIES, YOU EFFECTIVELY HAVE NO TOP PRIORITIES."
> —STEPHEN COVEY

Because of the pressure at work to keep things moving quickly, Celine worked late, came home to watch the news about the health crisis, and went to sleep late. She developed a negative attitude and became short and rude in her communication with others. She had the capacity to be a great leader but was on a downward spiral due to stress. I explained to her that self-care is not a suggestion for high performance, it's a requirement.

We started by looking at her daily routine, to find ways for her to refuel. Though somewhat skeptical that developing a routine would make much of an impact, she was willing to try. The three changes she built into her daily routine were:

1. Journaling 20 minutes a day about what she was grateful for.

2. Exercising in the morning in nature, before work.

3. Getting to bed no later than 10:30 pm.

These simple changes are all shown through research to reduce stress, increase happiness, and improve productivity. Research from the University of Michigan, published in *Journal of Happiness Studies*[67], indicates that "As little as 10 minutes of physical activity per week or 1 day of doing exercise per week might result in increased levels of happiness." And *Harvard Business Review*[68] reported, "When we think about the value of exercise, we tend to focus on the physical benefits ... But over the past decade, social scientists have quietly amassed compelling evidence suggesting that there is another, more immediate benefit of regular exercise: its impact on the way we think."

Within two weeks of Celine implementing her new daily routine, she told me, "I feel energized and focused again. Work is still really intense, but I feel more equipped to manage it." Creating a daily rhythm helped calm her, gave her back a sense of control over some aspects of her life, and made it possible for her to more effectively problem-solve at work.

Great leaders sitting in the middle chair develop this CARD**S**™ skill. The topic of stress, anxiety, resilience, and mental health is a priority for many organizations. The key is to equip leaders at every level with effective tools to manage their emotions. This may include creating a high-performance daily routine, differentiating between thoughts and feelings, listening to your feelings yet focusing your energy on healthy thoughts and actions, and prioritizing self-care, which not only will reduce stress and anxiety, but will also increase productivity.

Chapter 9 Action Steps: Apply the learning! Complete the exercise in *The Three Chairs: Workbook* & *Team Discussion Questions*. Go to www.dkleadership.org/thethreechairs for these bonus tools.

PART III

THE IMPACT
OF GREAT
LEADERSHIP ON AN
ORGANIZATION

When people within an organization focus on developing The 5 Leadership EQ Skills™ to sit in the middle chair (CARDS™), there is a positive ripple effect across the whole organization. When one person becomes a better leader, those new skills—communication, attitude, relationship, decision-making and stress-management—impact everyone around them. People feel equipped, listened to, understood and acknowledged. Ongoing feedback becomes the norm. Problems are quickly addressed and solved between individuals without involving HR. Top priorities are identified. Self-care is encouraged and modeled, stress is reduced. Delegation is prioritized. As a result, communication, engagement, productivity and retention all increase.

Great leadership offers a domino effect of positive efforts that can transform an entire company.

10

INCREASING RETENTION, EMPLOYEE ENGAGEMENT, AND TEAM COMMUNICATION

"Great teams do not hold back with one another. They are unafraid to air their dirty laundry. They admit their mistakes, their weaknesses, and their concerns without fear of reprisal."

—Patrick Lencioni, author of *The Five Dysfunctions of a Team: A Leadership Fable*

Several years ago, I consulted with an investment company that had recently rolled out a new management training program. The new initiative involved recruiting talent from top business schools and putting them through a multi-faceted program that rotated them through several business units. Many of the new hires started during the summer but within a few months began exiting the company. Given the time and resources devoted to creating and debuting this new program, the organization wanted to understand what was going wrong. I was hired to help determine why so many high performers were quitting so quickly.

I started with one of the most recent former employees, Brad, a bright, 25-year-old recent MBA grad, who agreed to a quasi-exit interview with me by phone. He told me he had joined the company in September and quit in December; we spoke in January, not long after his departure.

When I asked why he left, I expected to hear that he was dissatisfied with the work, didn't get along with his immediate supervisor, didn't feel challenged, or didn't like the culture. That wasn't it. The reason Brad left was that he had received little to no feedback between September and December. "My manager said, 'Here's your project. Let me know when it's done.'"

As he told the story with a lot of passion, I had an "aha" moment, and quickly understood the disconnect. If you are a boomer or Gen X, you may not see the problem. If you are a millennial you likely will get it. You will also then know why Brad said, "Honestly, Karyn, I felt completely abandoned." I empathized and asked for his permission to share this powerful insight with the HR team, to which he agreed.

The problem was significant due to generational differences. Many of the managers and supervisors employed at this investment company were Gen Xers and boomers—generations that typically value a management style that is highly independent—while their new hires were millennials, who often prefer a management style that is more collaborative with ongoing feedback. They want to do a great job and also want guidance to confirm they're delivering what their bosses are expecting.

The failure at this organization was not equipping and training their managers about these generational preferences. This ended up costing their bottom line, not to mention damaging their culture. Research in the *Harvard Business Review*[69] reported that employee turnover is extensive and the average cost is 21 percent of the employee's annual salary. So, failing to train Brad's manager cost this company $25,000, when all he wanted was ongoing feedback from his manager—a "work perk" that was free.

Research has consistently shown that employee engagement is closely linked with feedback. A study published in *Forbes*[70] states that 22,719 leaders who ranked in the bottom 10 percent based on their ability to give honest feedback, received engagement scores from their team members at 25 percent, while leaders ranked in the top 10 percent for giving honest feedback had team members rank them at 77 percent in engagement. The takeaway? Great leaders, sitting in the middle chair, give honest and regular feedback.

WHY PERFORMANCE REVIEWS ARE INEFFECTIVE FOR GIVING FEEDBACK TO HIGH-PERFORMING TEAMS

Ongoing feedback is essential for high engagement and retention in all teams. The challenge is that too many organizations hide behind their annual performance reviews in providing feedback. Many managers are nervous to give it and employees are anxious to receive it in this formal way. It's often a lose-lose situation. If your goal is to develop great leaders, problem-solve issues fast, and perform at a high level, teams need to be able to deal with issues as quickly as possible to correct it. If teams are relying on annual performance reviews to bring up issues, it's too late and, actually, unfair. Too often managers get upset with a team member's performance but don't tell them anything throughout the year, and then blindside the employee with a poor performance review.

People are not mind-readers. Great leaders, sitting in the middle chair, understand it is their responsibility to honestly communicate their expectations big and small, and provide feedback to their team. If companies really want to maintain giving performance reviews, they need to do the following:

1. Anything in the review should have already been brought up, so there are no surprises and the performance review is more of a formality.

2. Prioritize ongoing informal feedback in addition to the performance review, so it's not either/or, but rather *both*.

The Secret to Giving Ongoing Feedback

"A real leader uses every issue, no matter how serious and sensitive, to ensure that at the end of the debate we should emerge stronger and more united than ever before."
—Former President of South Africa, Nelson Mandela

To improve and master any skill, we need ongoing feedback to course-correct quickly. But how? For many leaders, giving ongoing feedback seems like one more thing to do, when their teams already have heavy workloads. First, change your mindset. When you learn to give informal feedback quickly, it takes only a little time on-the-spot—maybe one to five minutes—but will save you enormous time in the big picture, since you are problem-solving quickly. This will reserve your energy and drive your teams' productivity.

Second, learn how to give feedback. Many teams simply don't know how, which is a common problem. I recommend you use our tool called **The 3S's of Feedback™,** which consists of:

- **Soon**. As soon as someone is in need of instruction, tell them ASAP how to correct course. Immediacy is important. Keep the communication informal.

- **Short**. Feedback is great when it is short and to-the-point. Think of it more like a tweet, or a very short, informal conversation. Make it one to five minutes, tops.

- **Specific**. Focus first on what they are doing well, and then tell them specifically what you want them to do instead.

EXAMPLE MANAGER TO TEAM MEMBER (TIME: 3 MINUTES)

If you are a manager, feedback to a team member might go something like this:

You: "Hey, Jade, do you have a second to chat about that report you're preparing?"

Jade: "Of course. What are your thoughts?"

You: "You have a great mind for detail, that's why you're so good at this job. Instead of focusing so much on the financial data, I think you should incorporate more marketing, operations, and human resource statistics—to even out the picture of the company as a whole, beyond just sales and expenses. Does that make sense?"

Jade: "Yes, I think so."

You: "All you really need to do is cut a few paragraphs about the financial data and add others about marketing, human resources, and operational performance. What do you think? Do you need any help with that data?"

Jade: "Thanks, that's really helpful. I can do that."

You: "I know you can. I can't wait to see it!"

Great leaders in the middle chair understand that engagement and retention is highly connected to giving and receiving honest and ongoing feedback.

ORGANIZATIONS ARE THE NEW
EXTENDED FAMILY

A CNBC report[71] discovered that 56 percent of employees stated that they spend more time with their work family than the one they go home to. Most importantly, HP found, "having a familial relationship with coworkers boosts productivity and feelings of well-being in the workplace." Similarly, Gallup's 2017 "State of the American Workplace"[72] reported that friendships with coworkers increase employees' levels of happiness and engagement, both of which are correlated with retention.

The impact that a work family can have on retention was never clearer to me than when I was asked to speak at two insurance conferences outside Toronto that were both about management and employee retention. As it happens, one conference sold out right away and had a wait list while the other struggled to secure attendees, and I was curious to know why. The difference turned out to be that the sold-out conference had encouraged attendees to bring their families along to the event, promising that while they would have training events for the employees, there would be fun activities for the kids and spouses during the day and parties all together at night.

Not surprisingly, that focus on family permeated the entire company. In fact, the employees shared with me over dinner, "We'll never leave," they said, "because we're like a family." They couldn't imagine finding another workplace where they would have such close, positive relationships with coworkers. Consequently, few employees ever did leave.

The other conference, however, hadn't thought to include families. The focus was purely on work, and that attracted a different—and much smaller—audience. "Work is work and family is family. We keep the two separate," the CEO of the company sponsoring that conference told me. While many boomers often value that separation, Gen X and millennials tend to value work/life balance and family, and want their workplace to be like an extended family. They prefer places where bosses are more like mentors, aunts, and uncles, and their family is welcome at events.

Some progressive companies are taking it one step further. Bosses like entrepreneur Chieh Huang, founder of the e-tailer Boxed, provide benefits that include paying for workers' weddings and kids' tuition. While this may seem extreme, the principle is the same. Great organizations understand the value of building authentic relationships, family-like community, to drive engagement and retention.

So what's behind this trend to make some organizations like the new extended family? There are many variables, such as:

- Gen X and millennials highly value balance, family, and relationships.

- Most employees spend the majority of their best hours at work.

- Work colleagues often "get" them—they share a similar interest in their industry—while employees may have nothing in common with their family of origin.

- Many employees today are emotionally and physically disconnected from their family of origin and are craving community.

MODERN WORKPLACES LOOK LIKE A HOME

In recent years, pre-COVID, there was a shift driven by the "dot com generation" to move away from cubicles and private offices. Organizations were attracting great talent by designing stylish workplaces, also known as the "anti-office." Just look at the workplaces of Google and Microsoft and you will see that many offices look more like a home: open common areas like a living room, employees working side-by-side at what looks like dining room tables, employees eating lunch together in the kitchen, and ping-pong tables in the game rooms. While many younger generations value this energetic design, many older generations prefer their corner office and privacy—often viewed as their badge of honor for years of service. But what about now? Which approach is better for productivity? For engagement? Open or closed design? It depends on your employees' preferences and tasks. For companies that are multi-generational, an open concept workspace for those who prefer an energetic vibe can work well, as long as there are also offices for privacy. Some companies are taking it one step further in the "both" approach, creating cubicles to maximize productivity, called "work zones," but designing a large, stylish open concept area, like a kitchen/living room/game room for lunch and breaks. These are also called "social zones."

Why is this approach gaining steam? Because research is suggesting that while the open concept is stylish, it may not be practical. It also does not mean employees in such workspaces are having more meaningful conversations. In fact, research published in the *Harvard Business Review*[73] found that organizations that

A FEW YEARS AGO I WAS ASKED TO BE THE MEDIA SPOKESPERSON FOR THE "EAT TOGETHER DAY" CAMPAIGN FOR LOBLAW COMPANIES LIMITED (CANADA'S LARGEST RETAILER). THE MOVEMENT WAS ENCOURAGING PEOPLE TO #EATTOGETHER AT WORK. WHY? BECAUSE WHILE 68 PERCENT OF PEOPLE ENJOY EATING LUNCH WITH THEIR COLLEAGUES, RESEARCH FROM DALHOUSIE UNIVERSITY[75] FOUND THAT 39 PERCENT EAT ALONE AT THEIR DESKS. THERE ARE MANY BENEFITS TO EATING TOGETHER, ONE OF THEM BEING A GREAT WAY TO BUILD TEAM CULTURE, COMMUNITY AND REDUCE LONELINESS[76] (THE NEW EPIDEMIC IN AMERICA WHICH IMPACTS NEARLY HALF THE POPULATION). COMPANIES LIKE GOOGLE, WHICH SHOWED THEIR SUPPORT DURING THIS #EATTOGETHER DAY, HAVE INGRAINED EATING TOGETHER IN THEIR CULTURE TO DRIVE BOTH ENGAGEMENT AND WELLNESS.

"switched to open offices, face-to-face interactions fell by 70 percent." And research published in *Forbes*[74] reported that "1 in 3 workers feel distractions and noise from open work spaces hinder their productivity."

A key variable of a great leader who sits in the middle chair is not seeing problems as all-or-nothing. Instead, great leaders get to the root of the problem and look for a "both" approach whenever possible. A great example of a "both" office design solution can include stylish common areas to connect with others and office spaces for privacy. Engagement and retention is about understanding what people value. Ask your teams what they need in a great work environment for them to be inspired, comfortable, and highly productive.

STRATEGIES FOR IMPROVING EMPLOYEE RETENTION

Progressive employers are pulling out all the stops to attract and retain high-performing employees. They are applying a multi-pronged approach to engage them and keep them, by fostering personal relationships among employees and ensuring employees are constantly challenged at work. The three key elements to this retention plan are **The 3C's of Retention™:**

- **Communication**. Providing ongoing regular feedback to employees, to let them know what they've executed well and where they could adjust their approach, is critical for engagement and retention. Research from Gallup[77] found that 98 percent of employees will be disengaged if managers give little to no feedback.

- **Culture**. One of the most important ways to build culture is to create a place of community. As previously mentioned, the workplace is becoming the new extended family, which should be reflected in management style and workplace environment. Focus heavily on relationships and train new managers on this.

Research from Gallup[78] found "Managers account for at least 70 percent of variance in employee engagement." The problem is that many managers are not properly trained for these roles. Research cited in *Harvard Business Review*[79] reported that a staggering "50–60 percent of executives fail within the first 18 months of being promoted or hired."

- **Challenge**. Employees are hungry to learn. The more opportunities for growth you give, the more likely they will stay. An article in *Forbes*[80] shared that "An employer who doesn't focus on learning is going to lose out—in performance, engagement and retention." According to LinkedIn's 2018 Workforce Learning Report[81], a whopping 93 percent of employees would stay at a company longer if it invested in their careers."

Great leaders who sit in the middle chair, prioritize giving regular feedback to their teams, create a place of belonging—a new extended family—equip their new managers about the importance of culture, and communicate career opportunities for their employees. These are the elements that drive engagement and retention in their teams.

Chapter 10 Action Steps: Apply the learning! Complete the exercise in *The Three Chairs: Workbook & Team Discussion Questions*. Go to www.dkleadership.org/thethreechairs for these bonus tools.

11

THE CASE FOR WELLNESS– REDUCING STRESS, BURNOUT, AND INCREASING RESILIENCE

"Sleep deprivation reduces our emotional intelligence,
self-regard, assertiveness, sense of independence,
empathy toward others, the quality of our interpersonal
relationships, positive thinking, and impulse control."

—Arianna Huffington, author of *Thrive: The
Third Metric to Redefining Success and Creating
a Life of Well-Being, Wisdom, and Wonder*

James was the CEO of the family business his father had started and felt indebted to his dad after being handed control of the company in his mid-30s. He wanted to do a great job for his father. And in effort to accomplish that, James did more than any normal human being should be expected to do. He said "yes" to nearly everything anyone asked of him. Speak at an upcoming industry conference? Of course. Look over his CMO's PowerPoint presentation. Sure! As a result, his boundaries were out of whack, because they were almost nonexistent.

When we first met, I asked James to identify his vision and goal. His vision was "To be a great leader, husband, and father, and to grow the family business by 20 percent." I asked how he was doing according to his vision. "Failing miserably," he quickly responded. His sleep was severely lacking. His near-obsession with his job was negatively impacting all of his relationships. His marriage was "non-existent," his kids avoided him (complaining he was "always angry"), his senior leadership team voiced frustration because he was sending emails in the late evening, and the company was struggling. James was exhausted and headed toward burnout.

James was bright with a high IQ but bounced between all three chairs. He had a great vision and goals (middle chair), but he was executing, communicating and making decisions from the left and right chairs. Why? There were several reasons, but his three biggest roadblocks were:

- He had no clear boundaries between "work" and "home."

- He had an unrealistic mindset, believing that "If I say no, I'm weak and not a high achiever."

- He didn't like to delegate, believing "No one can do it like I can. If I delegate too much, I will be replaceable," which is a common fear among senior leaders.

I then asked him to describe his strategy for achieving his vision. He started explaining his plan for his business, which wasn't what I meant. I asked him to take it from a 50,000-foot view down to earth, down to what he could control. He wasn't sure how to do that.

To be a great leader, you need to start with self-leadership. Get yourself energized so you can give more to your family at home and your team at work. Without this as your foundation, you risk burnout in all parts of your life. Great leaders, sitting in the middle chair, understand this leadership principle.

I recommended that James first redesign his daily routine, so that he could create high performance work habits and refueling boundaries. This should be everyone's first step. Focus on creating three boundary zones: 1) time for high-level strategic thinking without interruptions, often mornings are often good for this; 2) time for teamwork, when meetings and delegation activities occur, often best in midmornings and afternoons; and 3) time to refuel, during the evening, to reconnect with family and friends, with technology turned off.

Creating these boundaries gave James the structure to do high-quality work and enabled him to delegate to his team. At first, James was unmotivated to delegate to others because he believed he was the only one who could do the work. This attitude was short-sighted and created a roadblock that was keeping him from his vision of being a great leader. Once he understood the cost of that mindset, he was able to start making some changes.

Next, James worked on his desire to win his father's approval, which is quite common in family business leaders. The reason it's a trap is that we cannot control it, which drives our anxiety. Instead, James needed to focus on what he could control—i.e., his own attitude and actions. He needed to aim to be a great leader, husband, and father, so that *he* was proud of his efforts; if his father approved, that would be a bonus, but if he didn't, James could still be proud of himself.

After only a few days, James's stress started to decrease. He was more productive, and he could relax at night guilt-free, he said. His team, especially younger managers, liked their new responsibilities because they had been getting bored, and their boss's mood was calmer. His young kids clearly noticed, as they made comments such as, "Dad we really like the new you." He started reconnecting with his wife by taking evening walks with their dog together. James was making incredible progress towards his vision.

THE CULTURE AND EMOTIONAL PULSE OF THE WORKFORCE

James's story embodies the problematic culture and emotional epidemic of the workforce. An article in *Psychology Today*[82] (pre-COVID) stated, "U.S. Leads in the Worldwide Anxiety Epidemic," citing research from the Gallup World Emotions Report[83]. Research from the Yale Center of Emotional Intelligence[84], found that one in five "highly engaged" workers were experiencing some kind of burnout. An article in *Fast Company*[85] tells the story of a former lawyer who eloquently said, "There are a lot of messages set up very early for us about what it means to be successful, and what it means to be a high achiever, and what it means to do well in life... What I'm not hearing are balanced messages around 'you need to take a break' or 'perfectionism should not be your standard.'"

What causes burnout? The World Health Organization[86] says, "Burn-out is a syndrome conceptualized as resulting from chronic workplace stress that has not been successfully managed." An article from the *Washington Post*[87] says that "95 percent of human resource leaders say burnout is sabotaging workplace retention, often because of overly heavy workloads."

So, let's start with the end in mind to tackle this topic of employee wellness head-on. What is your goal? Is it similar to James's: "To be a great leader, great partner, great parent, great friend?" How would you rate yourself (on a scale of zero to ten) according to your vision? What are your roadblocks? There are many—but here are four common ones:

> "PROGRESS IS MORE IMPORTANT THAN PERFECTION."
> —SIMON SINEK, AUTHOR OF *START WITH WHY: HOW GREAT LEADERS INSPIRE EVERYONE TO TAKE ACTION*

PROBLEM #1 FOR INDIVIDUALS: PERFECTIONISM

A common problem is the perfectionistic mindset, represented by the left or right chairs, that you shouldn't set boundaries, take breaks, ask for help, say no, or do anything less than perfect. This unrealistic attitude often fuels anxiety, stress, depression, and exhaustion—which can lead to performance problems, including irritability in communication, procrastination, low motivation, difficulty making decisions, mistakes on the job—and burnout. Perfection is an impossible goal that wreaks havoc on your emotional well-being.

PROBLEM #2 FOR INDIVIDUALS: STIGMA

High-achieving leaders often feel inadequacy around their inability to work through their problems. There is a lot of shame and embarrassment around problems at work caused by thoughts like, "I was the top of my (law, MBA, medical) program. Why can't I figure this out on my own?" or "I've always been an independent high-achiever and now I'm failing." This mindset keeps people suffering in silence.

PROBLEM #3 FOR ORGANIZATIONS: NOT KNOWING THE COST OF A LACK OF WELLNESS

When I speak at conferences about why wellness programs are critical to high-performing teams, I immediately see the audience's body language change. Facial expressions get stiff and shoulders go up. The mindset seems to be that wellness is the enemy of productivity, although science teaches us the opposite—that wellness can complement productivity. In fact, employee wellness is correlated positively or negatively with productivity, engagement, injuries, retention, and absenteeism. For example:

- Research from Stanford University[88] found that productivity drops sharply after employees hit a 50-hour workweek and has been connected to absenteeism and employee turnover.

- Research from the National Institute for Occupational Safety and Health (NIOSH) published in *Inc.*[89] cited that "in companies with high overtime, 54 percent had absentee rates above 9 percent" and "productivity declines by as much as 25 percent."

PROBLEM #4 FOR ORGANIZATIONS: MISUNDERSTANDING BETWEEN EXTERNAL AND INTERNAL WELLNESS PROGRAMS

Many organizations have wellness programs but find them ineffective because they are not addressing the root causes of burnout. Research from the University of California and Acadia University, published in *Harvard Business Review*[90] has indicated that burnout may be caused by: (1) workload (2) team relationships—community, fairness, values mismatch and (3) perceived lack of control and reward. There are two categories of wellness programs, external and internal, and both are important. Which type (s) do you have?

External Wellness Programs: Offer relief yet are like a band-aid to a problem if internal wellness topics are not in place. Examples include:

- Cool offices with nap rooms

- On-site fitness centers

- Newest technology for remote offices

Internal Wellness Programs: Deal with the root stressors and focus on:

- **Workloads/Time Management:** Programs to teach all levels of leaders how to prioritize, manage time effectively for high performance, delegate tasks, and ask for help.

- **Team/Relationships:** Programs to teach all levels of leaders, but especially managers, how to motivate, problem solve, give and receive feedback, and understand differences among people.

- **Individual/Control:** Programs to teach all levels of leaders how to set boundaries, say no, focus on excellence not perfection, and prioritize self-care for high performance.

External wellness perks are great, but understand that if your manager puts you down in front of your team and expects you to work 24/7, your newest technology means little-to-nothing. It won't convince employees to stay. Organizations need both internal and external wellness programs.

SIX SOLUTIONS TO PRIORITIZE WELLNESS

There are many ways you can improve wellness. First, if you are struggling with any type of anxiety, depression, or stress, see your family doctor right away to address your physical needs. Also ask for a referral to a solution-focused counselor to address your emotional needs. In addition, here are six solutions to get you started.

SOLUTION #1: BUILD A RESILIENT MINDSET

Although it is impossible to eliminate stress entirely, you can develop internal emotion-management tools that you can control which will reduce stress, such as through improved time management and sleep. This can help you build a resilient mindset. What is resilience? The American Psychological Association[91] says resilience is "the process of adapting well in the face of adversity, trauma, tragedy, threats or significant sources of stress ... resilience involves 'bouncing back' from these difficult experiences ... While these adverse events, much like rough river waters, are certainly painful and difficult, they don't have to determine the outcome of your life. There are many aspects of your life you can control, modify and grow with. That's the role of resilience."

SOLUTION #2: FOCUS ON WHAT YOU CAN CONTROL, ACCEPT WHAT YOU CANNOT

To learn new emotion-management tools, the first step is answering these two questions as they relate to your situation.

(1) What can you control? Your attitude and actions. Focus 100 percent of your energy and time here.

(2) What can you not control? Other people and external events. Accept this.

Many people focus on #2, or what they can't control, instead of #1, what they can control, which only increases stress and anxiety. It is much more effective to flip the focus and put all your energy on #1.

SOLUTION #3: IDENTIFY THE STRESSORS AND CREATE A PLAN TO TACKLE IT

Differentiate between stress and stressors. Stress is the feeling while stressor is the external circumstance. While you can't control feeling stress, you can control how you respond to the stressor. For example, if your stressor is workload, focus on how you can manage your time more effectively, say no, delegate, and ask for help. Do not get stuck focusing on problems and playing the victim, which is what people in the left and right chairs do. Leaders in the middle chair acknowledge how they feel, which is stress, yet focus on what they can control, create a plan, and charge toward it.

SOLUTION #4: PRIORITIZE TIME-MANAGEMENT TOOLS

If you want to radically decrease your stress, prioritize these time-management best practices:

A. **Maximize Your Energy and Time:** Design a high-performance daily routine with focus time, teamwork/delegating and refueling. This structure helps set boundaries.

B. **Set Boundaries and Say No:** Boundaries improve productivity and reduce stress. Train yourself to say "yes" to your priorities and "no, thank you" to everything else.

C. **Ask for Help:** If your workload seems unrealistic, talk with your manager or partner, and ask for help. This is a sign of a great leader and a team player in the middle chair.

D. **Delegate:** Research from Gallup[92] found that 70 percent of the workforce is not working to its full potential. It takes time to delegate, but will ultimately save you time. Effective delegation reduces stress and increases engagement. It's a win-win.

SOLUTION #5: PRIORITIZE SELF-CARE AND TOP THREE REFUELS

Once you've focused on your high-performance daily routine to be productive in your working hours, focus on identifying your top three refuels in your off-work hours. The higher your perfor-

> "VULNERABILITY SOUNDS LIKE TRUTH AND FEELS LIKE COURAGE. TRUTH AND COURAGE AREN'T ALWAYS COMFORTABLE, BUT THEY'RE NEVER WEAKNESS."
> —BRENÉ BROWN, *DARING GREATLY: HOW THE COURAGE TO BE VULNERABLE TRANSFORMS THE WAY WE LIVE, LOVE, PARENT, AND LEAD*

mance at work, the more you need to strategically structure your daily refuels to renew. The most common solutions often

> WE ARE HUMANS, NOT ROBOTS. ALL HIGH PERFORMERS NEED TO PRIORITIZE THEIR SELF-CARE. IT'S NOT A SUGGESTION—IT'S A REQUIREMENT.

include exercise, sleep, meditation, yoga, walking in nature, listening to music, cooking, sports, time with your pets, reading, and connecting with friends or family. Prioritize your top three to do daily.

SOLUTION #6: DEVELOP AN INTERNAL AND EXTERNAL WELLNESS PROGRAM

Talk with your HR department about your current wellness program. What are the wellness needs of your emerging leaders, managers, and senior leaders? An article in *Harvard Business Review*[93] says that external wellness perks, such as onsite massages to offset stress, can appear as "indulgent bribes to make up for the demanding expectations" if internal wellness needs, such as setting boundaries and setting realistic deadlines, are not taught and encouraged by organizations. Strategize to develop an internal and external wellness program with some of the ideas mentioned earlier.

A fast-growing real estate investment company in San Francisco asked our company to help them with this type of solution a few years ago. They wanted us to create a comprehensive leadership and wellness coaching program that could be used to equip their remote teams, especially their managers, across several states. We got to work and created a live online coaching program to make leadership development easy and save HR time. It's called "SI" (Success Intelligence with Dr. Karyn) and includes live online masterclasses and courses (especially for managers but suitable for all levels of leaders) that teach practical leadership and wellness tools. Our clients love it because it's engaging, digestible like a TED Talk and customizable like Netflix. Today SI is used by thousands of global leaders and professionals across many different industries, from finance and insurance, to accounting, engineering and healthcare, to name a few. What we have found interesting is that while many of our global clients position it to their teams as a leadership program, others prefer to use SI as a wellness program, because SI teaches dozens of stress-reducing tools, such as dealing with conflict, building resilience, setting boundaries, and time-management.

Research shows that leadership and wellness are highly interconnected; when you improve one, it often improves the other. For example, if a manager learns leadership tools to effectively give feedback or problem-solve issues within their team—productivity and communication will increase while stress and anxiety decrease.

Great leaders, sitting in the middle chair, prioritize wellness for themselves and their team. They care deeply for their people and encourage them to prioritize high performance habits, such as creating a daily routine to maximize productivity, delegating, and setting boundaries. They also encourage refueling during off-work hours, which increases productivity and decreases stress.

Chapter 11 Action Steps: Apply the learning! Complete the exercise in *The Three Chairs: Workbook* & *Team Discussion Questions*. Go to www.dkleadership.org/thethreechairs for these bonus tools.

12

DRIVING EMPLOYEE PRODUCTIVITY AND BUILDING CULTURE

"Gratitude drives happiness. Happiness boosts productivity. Productivity reveals mastery. And mastery inspires the world."

—Robin S. Sharma, author of *The Monk Who Sold His Ferrari*, *The 5AM Club*, and *The Leader Who Had No Title*

The purpose of this book is to identify HOW great leaders, who sit in the middle chair, develop The 5 Leadership EQ Skills™ (CARDS™) to drive their team's communication, productivity, and engagement. So now let's broaden your lens, connect the dots, and briefly define your WHAT. What is your definition of success? What are your goals as a high performer, team leader, and organization? After coaching hundreds of individuals, teams, and organizations, I saw a pattern—what I call the 6P's.

THE 6P'S OF ENGAGEMENT™ TO DRIVE YOUR PRODUCTIVITY AND BUILD CULTURE

Think of it like a metaphor. If I'm your coach and you are on the field, The 6P's of Engagement™ comprise your definition of success—the end goal—your WHAT. The 5 Leadership EQ Skills™ (CARDS™) are the tools—the how—to get you there. That's why productivity, engagement, and emotional intelligence are highly correlated. Research published in the Social Science Research Network (SSRN)[94] found that "success of any organization largely depends upon its productive workforce. Research has demonstrated that emotional intelligence plays a significant role in influencing the performance and productivity of employees at workplace."

See our diagram to show how The 5 Leadership EQ Skills™ of great leaders, who sit in the middle chair, drive The 6P's of Engagement™ for teams and organizations.

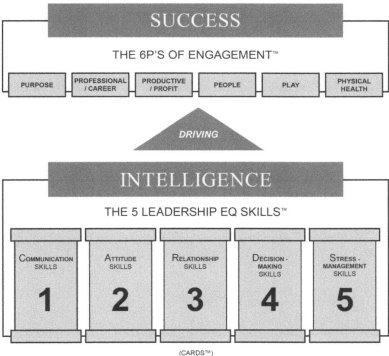

Here is an overview of The 6P's of Engagement™ and examples of how great leaders and great teams, sitting in the middle chair, prioritize the 6P's to drive productivity and build culture.

PURPOSE

Start with why. What is your purpose as a leader, team, and organization? Great leaders communicate purpose continuously. Purpose drives motivation, engagement, and feeds the soul. Simon Sinek says it well in his book, *Start with Why: How Great Leaders Inspire Everyone to Take Action,* when he says "All organizations start with WHY, but only the great ones keep their WHY clear year after year." Purpose is important because humans want to know that they're making a difference in some way. An article in the *Harvard Business Review*[95] cited research that employees who see their work as meaningful are 69 percent less likely to quit their jobs within the next six months. Purpose matters.

What are your purpose goals, in the next 365 days, to drive productivity and culture? Here are some examples from other great leaders, teams and organizations, sitting in the middle chair:

Individuals/High Performers: "To start mentoring."

Cultivating Team Culture: "To volunteer as a team with Habitat for Humanity."

Cultivating Company Culture: "To make sure when hiring that candidates share our company values and purpose."

PROFESSIONAL GROWTH

Career development and ongoing education drive engagement and culture. Great leaders develop their people. They show team members potential career paths to progress and then provide opportunities and training. Research from LinkedIn's 2019 Workforce Learning Report, published in *CNBC*[96], found that 94 percent of employees would stay longer with their employers if they invested in career development and helping them learn. More Gartner[97] research surveying 7,000 employees found that

"70 percent said they haven't mastered the skills they need for their jobs today" and "80 percent said they lack both the skills they need both for their current role and their future career." To drive productivity, engagement, and culture, organizations need to prioritize professional and career growth.

What are your professional goals, in the next 365 days, to drive productivity and culture? Here are some examples from other great leaders, teams and organizations, sitting in the middle chair:

Individuals/High Performers: "To work on my MBA part-time."

Cultivating Team Culture: "To provide new managers "Coaching Style" management training, to learn how to avoid team micro-managing and get employees to set goals and self-assess."

Cultivating Company Culture: "To provide leadership training for all employees."

PROFIT

> "PEOPLE WHO REPEATEDLY FIND CAREER SUCCESS LEARN TO BROADEN THEIR PERSPECTIVE AND UNDERSTAND THAT THERE ARE ALWAYS SEVERAL ROADS TO GETTING WHERE YOU WANT TO GO."
> —CARLA HARRIS, AUTHOR OF *EXPECT TO WIN: PROVEN STRATEGIES FOR SUCCESS FROM A WALL STREET VET*

Great leaders ensure their team is fairly compensated, though engagement isn't all about money. Fair compensation might mean paying out a bonus when the team hits a set goal, allowing employees to work from home more, or granting more vacation hours for a job well done.

Great leaders and organizations understand that

when this element is not addressed, people may leave. Research published in *CNBC*[98] reported that the average raise is three percent, yet *Forbes*[99] says a raise has to be significantly larger for someone to consider a new job since "the average raise an employee receives for leaving is between a 10 percent to 20 percent increase in salary."

The key with this 6P is a well-rounded compensation package. An article in the *Wall Street Journal*[100] stated that organizations should "get current data on industry pay packages, and get creative when necessary with benefits, flexible work schedules and bonus structures … Pay attention to employees' personal needs and offer more flexibility where you can."

What are your profit goals, in the next 365 days, to drive productivity and culture? Here are some examples from other great leaders, teams and organizations, sitting in the middle chair:

> **Individuals/High Performers:** "To have a conversation with my director about the skills I need to hone this next year to qualify for a raise."

> **Cultivating Team Culture:** "To discuss with my team what they value when targets get met (paid bonuses, extra vacation days, other perks)."

> **Cultivating Company Culture:** "To increase our employee retention (and therefore profit) from 75 to 80 percent."

People

A couple of years ago, a highly profitable and growing multi-location healthcare company was struggling with productivity, engagement, and retention. They were hiring millennials but weren't able to hold onto them. "We keep throwing more money at them and they are not staying," the CEO revealed. A boomer herself, who values money, she was looking at the situation from her lens and not seeking to understand her team. Compensation is very important and needs to be fair, but profit is only one of the 6P's that drive engagement and retention. It's important to assess the other 5P's to uncover what need is missing. When she truly stopped to process this information, it became clear that her managers did not know how to effectively manage. That's why employees were leaving. Her managers needed to develop their 5 Leadership EQ Skills™. Gallup Research[101] found that 50 percent of employees leave their jobs to get away from their manager. It continues to say, published in *Harvard Business Review*[102] "The best managers make a concerted effort to get to know their employees and help them feel comfortable talking about any subject, whether it is work related or not. A productive workplace is one in which people feel safe—safe enough to experiment, to challenge, to share information and to support one another." Building a great culture assures employees at all levels that they can make a mistake and they won't be punished for it. This reflects the anti-perfectionism mindset. They can make errors, forget things—or commit any variation of failure—and they won't be demoted or lose their job.

What are your people goals, in the next 365 days, to drive productivity and culture? Here are some examples from other great leaders, teams and organizations, sitting in the middle chair:

Individuals/High Performers: "To get involved in my company's Employee Resource Group (ERG) and meet other employees who are passionate about equity, inclusion, and diversity."

Cultivating Team Culture: "To have weekly meetings to access workloads and priorities, and monthly potlucks (or virtual lunches) to connect as a team."

Cultivating Company Culture: "To host monthly company-wide meetings that will include recognizing great managers and great teams."

PLAY

Great leaders prioritize play and laughter as an important part of wellness and team bonding. It can be the reason an employee elects to stay put instead of quitting. A client was considering leaving his employer for another company because he was offered a

> "SUCCESSFUL PEOPLE ARE ALWAYS LOOKING FOR OPPORTUNITIES TO HELP OTHERS.
> UNSUCCESSFUL PEOPLE ARE ALWAYS ASKING, "WHAT'S IN IT FOR ME?"
> —BRIAN TRACY

slightly higher salary. Then he realized that if he left, he wouldn't be able to hang out with his colleagues on Thursdays at 4:00, when they had weekly, company-wide wine-and-cheese socials. He realized how much that connection, laughter, and community meant to him—and he declined the other offer. It was the people and play categories of the 6P's that kept him there.

Did you know that laughter when you play is one of the simplest ways for teams to bond? Research published in the *American Journal of Lifestyle Medicine*[103] cites many benefits of laughter, such as "improving affect, depression, anxiety, and stress." Play and laughter can work as social glue in building team culture. Research from the University of North Carolina, published in the *Greater Good Magazine: Science-Based Insights For A Meaningful Life*[104], found that "shared laughter signals that they see the world in the same way... Perceived similarity ends up being an important part of the story of relationships."

What are your play goals, in the next 365 days, to drive productivity and culture? Here are some examples from other great leaders, teams and organizations, sitting in the middle chair:

Individuals/High Performers: "To take a cooking class (and share it at our next team potluck)."

Cultivating Team Culture: "To give our team a "play" budget and brainstorm how we want to use it to strengthen our team's culture, through dinners, sporting events, or speakers, perhaps."

Cultivating Company Culture: "To host annual retreats for all employees and their families."

PHYSICAL HEALTH

Great leaders see team members holistically and recognize the power of wellness—physically, mentally, and emotionally. A *Forbes*[105] article states that "89 percent of workers at companies that support well-being initiatives are more likely to recommend their company as a good place to work" and the *American Psychological Association*[106] said that "less than half of working Americans (44 percent) say the climate in their organization supports employee well-being ... a key part of the solution is senior leadership support."

Organizations need to structure and encourage it, and employees need to prioritize it. Research by Oxford Economics as reported in *Forbes*[107] said more than 40 percent of employees who received paid time off, did not take their holiday. Why? Several reasons: heavy workloads, some managers dis-

> "A STUDY CONDUCTED AT HARVARD MEDICAL SCHOOL FOUND THAT PEOPLE WHO GOT MORE SLEEP THAN THE BARE MINIMUM THEY NEEDED INCREASED THE VOLUME OF GRAY MATTER IN THEIR BRAINS, WHICH IS LINKED TO IMPROVED PSYCHOLOGICAL HEALTH."
> —ARIANNA HUFFINGTON, AUTHOR OF *THRIVE: THE THIRD METRIC TO REDEFINING SUCCESS AND CREATING A LIFE OF WELL-BEING, WISDOM, AND WONDER*

couraged it, others were afraid that they would appear less dedicated. Great leaders in the middle chair understand that physical health and wellness is a requirement for high performance and needs to be prioritized for themselves and their team.

What are your physical health goals, in the next 365 days, to drive productivity and culture? Here are some examples from other great leaders, teams and organizations, sitting in the middle chair:

> **Individuals/High Performers:** "To get seven to eight solid hours of sleep each night."

> **Cultivating Team Culture:** "To start "walk and talk" meetings with my team and encourage my team to focus on efficiency, prime-time hours, and setting boundaries."

> **Cultivating Company Culture:** "To provide a wellness program for all of our employees and have senior leaders model this for high performance."

The more of these 6P's you can incorporate within your organization, the more you will drive your teams' productivity, engagement, and culture. Great leaders, sitting in the middle chair, identify their goals regarding The 6P's of Engagement™ and use their 5 Leadership EQ Skills™ (CARDS™) to achieve their greatest results as a team and organization.

Chapter 12 Action Steps: Apply the learning! Complete the exercise in *The Three Chairs: Workbook* & *Team Discussion Questions*. Go to www.dkleadership.org/thethreechairs for these bonus tools.

EPILOGUE AND BONUS RESOURCES

My purpose is developing great leaders. I want individuals and teams to not only learn about The Three Chairs and their impact on leadership but, most importantly, to take action so they can be more fully engaged, energized, happier, productive—reaching their greatest potential professionally and personally.

Great leaders sit in the middle chair. They know what success looks like as an individual, as a team, and as an organization. That is The 6P's of Engagement™, and they know how to continually develop The 5 Leadership EQ Skills™ (CARDS™) as the tools to get them there.

SPOTTING THE GREAT LEADERS AMONG US

Now that you know what it looks like to sit in The Three Chairs, you can more easily spot someone in the left chair who is struggling with insecurity, or the person in the right chair who is never wrong and puts others down, as well as the leader in the middle chair who lifts up those around them and respectfully voices opinions with strength and class. Recognizing the characteristics of a great leader is the first step on the path to becoming one yourself, regardless of your title, age, ethnicity, experience, or education. All of us are capable of learning how to sit in the middle chair. I hope that excites and inspires you.

THE LEADERSHIP JOURNEY

As I shared at the beginning that my leadership journey started in eighth grade. I learned that leadership and success is a journey, not a straight line. It's an exciting adventure met with lots of hills and valleys, roadblocks, construction, and detours. The key is keeping your eyes and mind focused on where you and your team want to go, being agile and having the courage to ask for feedback and directions along the way. If possible, don't take the journey alone. Find others, such as teams, business forums, coworkers, book club members, family, or friends, who are motivated to do the journey with you.

GETTING STARTED

So how can you get started? If you haven't done so yet, go to our website (www.dkleadership.org/thethreechairs) for many free bonus resources to get you started on your journey to sit in the middle chair as an individual, team, and organization.

(1) **For Individuals and Teams:** Get your free *The Three Chairs Workbook.* This resource is a great tool to provide step-by-step action steps for each chapter.

(2) **For Individuals and Teams:** Watch and read the free Q&A from others and be sure to send in your questions. *The Three Chairs* is a business book, but there are many applications for families, including marriages and parenting. The Q&A will cover both.

(3) **For Teams:** Get the free *The Three Chairs Discussion Questions.* Learning is the most effective when people can reflect, digest, and discuss the content.

(4) **For Individuals, Managers, Teams and Organizations:** If you need more practical leadership and wellness tools, check out our Live Online SI: Leadership Coaching Program. (www.dkleadership.org/about-si)

(5) For Individuals, Managers, Teams, and Organizations: What are your other needs that have not yet been addressed? Contact us (www.dkleadership.org). We'd love to help and are continually developing more practical resources to serve our global clients.

Take action. Start small. Be kind to yourself in the process. And I will see you in our DKL Community. I hope you feel more inspired and equipped. I look forward to journeying with you!

Sincerely,
Dr. Karyn

ENDNOTES

1   Chamorro-Premuzic, T. "Can You Really Improve Your Emotional Intelligence?" *Harvard Business Review*. (2013). https://hbr.org/2013/05/can-you-really-improve-your-em

2   Sakulku, J. "The Impostor Phenomenon." *The Journal of Behavioral Science*. (2011). https://so06.tci-thaijo.org/index.php/IJBS/article/view/521

3   Abele, A., & Spurk, D. "The Longitudinal Impact Of Self-Efficacy And Career Goals On Objective And Subjective Career Success." *Journal of Vocational Behavior*. (2009). https://www.sciencedirect.com/science/article/abs/pii/S0001879108000973

4   Lambertz-Berndt, M., & Blight, M. "You Don't Have To Like Me, But You Have To Respect Me: The Impacts of Assertiveness, Cooperativeness, And Group Satisfaction In Collaborative Assignments." *Business and Professional Communication Quarterly*. (2016). https://journals.sagepub.com/doi/10.1177/2329490615604749

5   Evez, A., & Judge, T. "Relationship Of Core Self-Evaluations To Goal-Setting, Motivation, And Performance." *Journal of Applied Psychology*. (2002). https://www.researchgate.net/publication/11589908_Relationship_of_Core_Self-Evaluations_to_Goal_Setting_Motivation_and_Performance

6   Graham, S.M., & Clark, M.S. "Self-Esteem And Organization Of Valenced Information About Others: The'Jekyll And Hyde'-ing Of Relationship Partners." *Journal of Personality and Social Psychology*. (2006). https://doi.apa.org/doiLanding?doi=10.1037%2F0022-3514.90.4.652

7   Fast, N., Burris, E., & Bartel, C. "Research: Insecure Managers Don't Want Your Suggestions." *Harvard Business Review*. (2014). https://hbr.org/2014/11/research-insecure-managers-dont-want-your-suggestions

8   Silverman, S., & McConnell, N. "Arrogance: A Formula For Leadership Failure." *The Industrial-Organizational Psychologist*. (2012). https://pdfs.semanticscholar.org/fa02/adc533042a33adcf2ac14576ef35b5589ceb.pdf

9   Bahns, A.J., Crandall, C.S., Gillath, O., & Preacher, K.J. "Similarity
    In Relationships As Niche Construction: Choice, Stability,
    And Influence Within Dyads In A Free Choice Environment. "
    Journal of Personality and Social Psychology. (2017). https://
    psycnet.apa.org/doiLanding?doi=10.1037%2Fpspp0000088

10 Xu, J., Liu, Y., & Chung, B. "Leader Psychological Capital And
    Employee Work Engagement: The Roles Of Employee Psychological
    Capital And Team Collectivism." *Leadership and Organizational
    Development Journal.* (2017). https://www.emerald.com/insight/
    content/doi/10.1108/LODJ-05-2016-0126/full/html

11 Avey, J., Wernsing, T., & Mhatre, K. "A Longitudinal Analysis Of
    Positive Psychological Constructs And Emotions On Stress, Anxiety,
    And Well-Being." *Journal of Leadership and Organizational Studies.*
    (2011). https://journals.sagepub.com/doi/10.1177/1548051810397368

12 Goleman, D. "What Makes a Leader." *Harvard Business Review.*
    (2004). https://hbr.org/2004/01/what-makes-a-leader

13 Oishi, S., Diener, E., & Lucas, R. "Value As A Moderator In
    Subjective Well-Being." *Journal of Personality.* (1999). https://
    www.semanticscholar.org/paper/Value-as-a-Moderator-
    in-Subjective-Well%E2%80%90Being-Oishi-Diener/
    df98a782523c0569f3b16fd1ae2f4dcaa87470b4

14 Achor, S. "The Value Of Happiness." *Harvard Business
    Review.* (2012). https://www.shawnachor.com/project/
    harvard-business-review-the-value-of-happiness/

15 Beck, R., & Harter, J. "The State Of The American Manager:
    Analytics And Advice For Leaders." *Gallup.* (2015). https://www.
    gallup.com/services/182138/state-american-manager.aspx

16 Kohll, A. "How Deloitte Is Addressing Employee Burnout With
    Real-Time Data." *Forbes.* (2019). https://www.forbes.com/sites/
    alankohll/2019/11/13/how-deloitte-is-addressing-employee-burnout-
    with-real-time-data/?sh=5d8ddb7f13f4

17 Santos, M. "Study Says Women Are More Likely To Experience Burnout
    Than Men. *National Association of Female Executives.* (2018). https://
    www.nafe.com/study-says-women-are-more-likely-to-experience-
    burnout-than-men

18 Fisher, J. "Workplace Burnout Survey." *Deloitte.* (2015). https://www2.
    deloitte.com/us/en/pages/about-deloitte/articles/burnout-survey.html

19 Wigert, B., & Agrawal, S. "Employee Burnout, Part 1: The
    5 Main Causes." *Gallup.* (2018). https://www.gallup.com/
    workplace/237059/employee-burnout-part-main-causes.aspx

20 Goleman, D. "The Feedback Loop." *Daniel Goleman's
    Blog.* (2012). https://www.goodreads.com/author/
    show/829.Daniel_Goleman/blog?page=19

21 Zenger, J., & Folkman, J. "Your Employees Want The Negative Feedback You Hate To Give." *Harvard Business Review*. (2014). https://hbr.org/2014/01/your-employees-want-the-negative-feedback-you-hate-to-give

22 Duhigg, C. "What Google Learned From Its Quest To Build The Perfect Team." *The New York Times*. (2016). https://www.nytimes.com/2016/02/28/magazine/what-google-learned-from-its-quest-to-build-the-perfect-team.html

23 Pelletier, L. G., & Vallerand, R. J. "Supervisors' Beliefs And Subordinates' Intrinsic Motivation: A Behavioral Confirmation Analysis." *Journal of Personality and Social Psychology*. (1996). https://doi.org/10.1037/0022-3514.71.2.331

24 Bijlsma, K., & Van De Bunt, G. "Antecedents Of Trust In Managers: A 'Bottom-Up' Approach." *Personnel Review*. (2003). https://www.emerald.com/insight/content/doi/10.1108/00483480310488388/full/html

25 "Lost-Worktime Injuries and Illnesses: Characteristics and Resulting Days Away from Work, 2001." *Bureau of Labor Statistics*. (2004). https://www.bls.gov/news.release/archives/osh2_03252004.pdf

26 Steelman, L., & Rutkowski, K. "Moderators Of Employee Reactions To Negative Feedback." *Journal of Managerial Psychology*. (2004). https://www.emerald.com/insight/content/doi/10.1108/02683940410520637/full/html

27 Caprino, K. "5 Communication Blunders That Could Get You Fired." *Forbes*. (2017). https://www.forbes.com/sites/kathycaprino/2017/08/28/5-communication-blunders-that-could-get-you-fired/?sh=2a84bb0c6963

28 Del Mar Ferradas, M., Freire, C., Nunez, J.C., & Regueiro, B. "Associations Between Profiles Of Self-Esteem And Achievement Goals And The Protection Of Self-Worth In University Students." *International Journal of Environmental Research and Public Health*. (2019). https://www.ncbi.nlm.nih.gov/pmc/articles/PMC6616880/

29 Price-Mitchell, M. "Goal-Setting Is Linked To Higher Achievement." *Psychology Today*. (2018). https://www.psychologytoday.com/us/blog/the-moment-youth/201803/goal-setting-is-linked-higher-achievement

30 Tabaka, M. "New Study Says This Simple Step Will Increase The Odds Of Achieving Your Goals." *Inc*. (2019). https://www.inc.com/marla-tabaka/this-study-found-1-simple-step-to-practically-guarantee-youll-achieve-your-goals-for-real.html

31 Seijts, G., Latham, G., Tasa, K., & Latham, B. "Goal-Setting And Goal Orientation: An Integration Of Two Different Yet Related Literatures." *Academy of Management Journal*. (2017). https://journals.aom.org/doi/10.5465/20159574

32 Bandura, A. "On The Functional Properties Of Perceived Self-Efficacy Revisited." *Journal of Management.* (2011). https://journals. sagepub.com/doi/10.1177/0149206311410606

33 Thulien, N., Wang, A., & Hwang, S. "Housing Stabilization: Testing The Link Between Identity And Socioeconomic Inclusion." *Canadian Observatory on Homelessness.* (2019). https://www. homelesshub.ca/researchmatters/the-Identity-Project

34 Schwantes, M. "Science Says Only 8 Percent Of People Actually Achieve Their Goals. Here Are 7 Things They Do Differently." *Inc.* (2018). https://www.inc.com/marcel-schwantes/ science-says- only-8-percent-of-people-actually-achieve-their-goals-here-are-7- things-they-do-differently.html

35 Grant, H. "How To Get The Help You Need." *Harvard Business Review.* (2018). https://hbr.org/2018/05/how-to-get-the-help-you-need

36 Mejia, Z. "This Simple Method Is Used by Bill Gates, Larry Page And Even Bono To Tackle Their Biggest Goals." CNBC. (2018). https:// www.cnbc.com/2018/08/14/this-goal-setting-method-is-used-by-bill-gates-larry-page-and-bono.html

37 Fratto, N. "3 Ways To Measure Your Adaptability—And How To Improve It." *TED.* (2019). https://www.ted.com/talks/natalie_fratto_3_ways_ to_measure_your_adaptability_and_how_to_improve_it#t-333138

38 Liu, J. "120 Million Workers Will Need Retraining Due To AI—But They May Already Have The Skills Employers Want Most." *CNBC.* (2019). https://www.cnbc.com/2019/09/10/120m-workers-need-retraining-but-many-already-have-skills-employers-want.html

39 Barsade, S., & O'Neill, O. "Employees Who Feel Love Perform Better." *Harvard Business Review.* (2014). https://hbr. org/2014/01/employees-who-feel-love-perform-better

40 Taylor, S. "5 Major Differences Between The Lives Of Millennials And Baby Boomers." *Business Insider.* (2019). https://www. businessinsider.com/difference-millennials-baby-boomers-2019-4

41 "Manager Of A Generation: Millennials Vs. Gen X." *King University Online.* https://online.king.edu/infographics/ manager-generation-millennials-vs-gen-x/

42 Renzulli, K.A. "28% Of Millennials Are Managers Now— Here Are 5 Ways They're Changing The Office." *CNBC.* (2019). https://www.cnbc.com/2019/03/05/5-ways-millennial-managers-are-changing-the-office.html

43 Asghar, R. "Study: Millennials Are The True Entrepreneur Generation." *Forbes.* (2014). https://www.forbes.com/ sites/robasghar/2014/11/11/ study-millennials-are-the-true-entrepreneur-generation/?sh=348c27a7 73dc

44 Eswaran, V. "The Business Case For Diversity In The Workplace Is Now Overwhelming." *World Economic Forum.* (2019). https://www.weforum.org/agenda/2019/04/business-case-for-diversity-in-the-workplace/

45 Lorenzo, R., Voigt, N., Tsusaka, M., & Krentz, M. "How Diverse Leadership Teams Boost Innovation." *Boston Consulting Group.* (2018). https://www.bcg.com/en-us/publications/2018/how-diverse-leadership-teams-boost-innovation

46 Scelfo, J. "A University Recognizes A Third Gender: Neutral." *The New York Times.* (2015). https://www.nytimes.com/2015/02/08/education/edlife/a-university-recognizes-a-third-gender-neutral.html?_r=0

47 Tamburin, A. "Colleges Trend Toward Gender-Neutral Pronouns." *USA Today.* (2015). https://www.usatoday.com/story/news/nation/2015/09/05/colleges-trend-toward-gender-neutral-pronouns/71780214/

48 45 Huynh, J. "Study Finds No Difference In The Amount Men And Women Talk." *University of Arizona.* (2014). https://ubrp.arizona.edu/study-finds-no-difference-in-the-amount-men-and-women-talk

49 Kinsey Gorman, C. "Is Your Communication Style Dictated By Your Gender?" *Forbes.* (2016). https://www.forbes.com/sites/carolkinseygoman/2016/03/31/is-your-communication-style-dictated-by-your-gender/?sh=6358d768eb9d

50 Harvard Unconscious Bias Test. https://implicit.harvard.edu/implicit

51 McIntosh, P. "White Privilege: Unpacking The Invisible Knapsack." *American Psychological Association.* (1998). https://psycnet.apa.org/record/1998-07624-010

52 Gerdeman, D. "Minorities Who 'Whiten' Job Resumes Get More Interviews." *Harvard Business School.* (2017). https://hbswk.hbs.edu/item/minorities-who-whiten-job-resumes-get-more-interviews

53 Barnes, C. "The Ideal Work Schedule, As Determined By Circadian Rhythms." *Harvard Business Review.* (2015). https://hbr.org/2015/01/the-ideal-work-schedule-as-determined-by-circadian-rhythms#:~:text=Humans%20have%20a%20well%2Ddefined,persistent%20circadian%20rhythms%20can%20be

54 Hofmann, W., Luhmann, M., Fisher, R., Vohs, K., & Baumeister, R. "Yes, But Are They Happy? Effects Of Trait Self-Control On Affective Well-Being And Life Satisfaction." *Journal of Personality.* (2014). https://pubmed.ncbi.nlm.nih.gov/23750741/

55 Abrams, L. "Study: People With A Lot Of Self-Control Are Happier." *The Atlantic.* (2013). https://www.theatlantic.com/health/archive/2013/07/study-people-with-a-lot-of-self-control-are-happier/277349

56 "Guide: Set Goals With OKRs." *Google.* https://rework.withgoogle.com/guides/set-goals-with-okrs/steps/introduction/

57 Howatt, B. "Learn How To Be A Leader Who Delegates." *Globe and Mail.* (2016). https://www.theglobeandmail.com/report-on-business/

careers/workplace-award/learn-how-to-be-a-leader-who-delegates/article33221222/

58 Damasio, A., & Carvalho, G. "The Nature Of Feelings: Evolutionary And Neurobiological Origins." *Nature Reviews Neuroscience.* (2013). https://www.nature.com/articles/nrn3403

59 Winerman, L. "Talking The Pain Away." *American Psychological Association.* (2006). https://www.apa.org/monitor/oct06/talking

60 Goleman, D. "Why Aren't We More Compassionate?" *TED.* (2007). https://www.ted.com/talks/daniel_goleman_why_aren_t_we_more_compassionate/transcript?language=en

61 Lee, B. "Here Are The 27 Different Human Emotions, According To A Study." *Forbes.* (2017). https://www.forbes.com/sites/brucelee/2017/09/09/here-are-the-27-different-human-emotions-according-to-a-study/?sh=647b5c931335

62 Escalante, A. "U.S. Leads In The Worldwide Anxiety Epidemic." *Psychology Today.* (2019). https://www.psychologytoday.com/ca/blog/shouldstorm/201904/us-leads-in-the-worldwide-anxiety-epidemic

63 Morin, A. "A New Study Says Anxiety Can Help You Perform Better-- But Only If You Know How to Respond To It." *Forbes.* (2017). https://www.forbes.com/sites/amymorin/2017/08/12/a-new-study-says-anxiety-can-help-you-perform-better-but-only-if-you-know-how-to-respond-to-it/?sh=910026a20f61

64 Kecmanovic, J. "A Psychologist's Science-Based Tips For Emotional Resilience During The Coronavirus Crisis." *Washington Post.* (2020). https://www.washingtonpost.com/lifestyle/wellness/anxiety-coronavirus- mental-wellness-tips/2020/03/16/f187faf2-67b8-11ea-9923- 57073adce27c_story.html

65 Tedeschi, R., & Calhoun, L. "Posttraumatic Growth: Conceptual Foundations And Empirical Evidence." *Psychological Inquiry.* (2009). https://www.tandfonline.com/doi/abs/10.1207/s15327965pli1501_01?casa_token=F3wNpSxnDOAAAAAA%3Ad-AZr4azHf5Iqs6UQ8NhU7_ZUrcbHSJCjMBrqEXycSD9do8GQLCUPsAwNtzEBSyc1WrygLMOrrPL&

66 Sherman, G., Lee, J., Cuddy, A., Renshon, J., Oveis, C., Gross, J., & Lerner, J. "Leadership Is Associated With Lower Levels Of Stress." *Psychological and Cognitive Sciences.* (2012). https://www.ncbi.nlm.nih.gov/pmc/articles/PMC3497788/

67 Zhang, Z., & Chen, W. "A Systematic Review Of The Relationship Between Activity And Happiness." *Journal of Happiness Studies.* (2019). https://www.researchgate.net/publication/323992118_A_Systematic_Review_of_the_Relationship_Between_Physical_Activity_and_Happiness

68 Friedman, R. "Regular Exercise Is Part of Your Job." *Harvard Business Review*. (2014). https://hbr.org/2014/10/regular-exercise-is-part- of-your-job

69 Chamberlain, A. "Why Do Employees Stay? A Clear Career Path And Good Pay, For Starters." *Harvard Business Review*. (2017). https://hbr.org/2017/03/why-do-employees-stay-a-clear-career-path-and-good-pay-for-starters

70 Folkman, J. "The Best Gift Leaders Can Give: Honest Feedback." *Forbes*. (2013). https://www.forbes.com/sites/joefolkman/2013/12/19/the-best-gift-leaders-can-give-honest-feedback/?sh=16398b454c2b

70 Umoh, R. "This Study Identified The 5 People That Make Up A 'Work Family'—Which One Are You?" *CNBC*. (2017). https://www.cnbc.com/2017/12/14/this-study-identified-the-5-people-that-make-up-a-work-family.html

72 Mejia, Z. "Why Having Friends At Work Will Make You A Better Employee." *CNBC*. (2017). https://www.cnbc.com/2017/08/16/why-having-friends-at-work-will-make-you-a-better-employee.html

73 Bernstein, E., & Waber, B. "The Truth About Open Offices." *Harvard Business Review*. (2019). https://hbr.org/2019/11/the-truth-about-open-offices

74 Wertz, J. "Open-Plan Work Spaces Lower Productivity And Employee Morale." *Forbes*. (2019). https://www.forbes.com/sites/jiawertz/2019/06/30/open-plan-work-spaces-lower-productivity-employee-morale/?sh=3cca738c61cd

75 Levesque, L. "Almost 40 Percent Of Canadians Eat Lunch At Their Desks, New Study Finds." *The Toronto Star*. (2017). https://www.thestar.com/life/2017/05/18/almost-40-per-cent-of-canadians-eat-lunch-at-their-desks-new-study-finds.html

76 Ninivaggi, F. "Loneliness: A New Epidemic In The USA." *Psychology Today*. (2019). https://www.psychologytoday.com/ca/blog/envy/201902/loneliness-new-epidemic-in-the-usa

77 Brim, B., & Asplund, J. "Driving Engagement By Focusing On Strengths." *Gallup*. (2009). https://news.gallup.com/businessjournal/124214/driving-engagement-focusing-strengths.aspx

78 Beck, R., & Harter, J. "Why Good Managers Are So Rare." *Harvard Business Review*. (2014). https://hbr.org/2014/03/why-good-managers-are-so-rare

79 Carucci, R. "Executives Fail To Execute Strategy Because They're Too Internally Focused." *Harvard Business Review*. (2017). https://hbr.org/2017/11/executives-fail-to-execute-strategy-because-theyre-too-internally-focused

80 Biro, M.. "Developing Your Employees Is The Key To Retention—Here Are 4 Smart Ways To Start." *Forbes*. (2018). https://www.forbes.com/

sites/meghanbiro/2018/07/23/developing-your-employees-is-the-key-to-retention-here-are-4-smart-ways-to-start/?sh=3f97f9ec3734

81 "2018 Workplace Learning Report." *LinkedIn Learning.* (2018). https://learning.linkedin.com/resources/workplace-learning-report-2018

82 Escalante, A. "U.S. Leads In the Worldwide Anxiety Epidemic." *Psychology* Today. (2019). https://www.psychologytoday.com/ca/blog/shouldstorm/201904/us-leads-in-the-worldwide-anxiety-epidemic

83 "Gallup 2019 Global Emotions Report." *Gallup.* (2019) https://www.gallup.com/analytics/248906/gallup-global-emotions-report-2019.aspx

84 Moeller, J., Ivcevic, Z., White, A., Menges, J., Brackett, M. "Highly Engaged But Burned Out: Intra-Individual Profiles In The US Workforce." *Career Development International.* (2018). https://www.emerald.com/insight/content/doi/10.1108/CDI-12-2016-0215/full/html

85 Purbasari Horton, A. "How Do You Know If You're About To Burn Out?" *Fast Company.* (2019). https://www.fastcompany.com/90311958/hhow-to-identify-and-overcome-burnout

86 "Burn-Out An "Occupational Phenomenon": International Classification Of Diseases." *World Health Organization.* (2019). https://www.who.int/news/item/28-05-2019-burn-out-an-occupational-phenomenon-international-classification-of-diseases

87 Rough, J. "From Moms To Medical Doctors, Burnout Is Everywhere These Days." *Washington Post.* (2019). https://www.washingtonpost.com/national/health-science/from-moms-to-medical-doctors-burnout-is-everywhere-these-days/2019/03/29/1cea7d92-401d-11e9-922c-64d6b7840b82_story.html

88 Sullivan, B. "Memo To Work Martyrs: Long Hours Make You Less Productive." *CNBC.* (2015). https://www.cnbc.com/2015/01/26/working-more-than-50-hours-makes-you-less-productive.html

89 Popomaronis, T. "Science Says You Shouldn't Work More Than This Number Of Hours A Week." *Inc.* (2016). https://www.inc.com/tom-popomaronis/science-says-you-shouldnt-work-more-than-this-number-of-hours-a-day.html

90 Saunders, E.G. "6 Causes Of Burnout, And How To Avoid Them." *Harvard Business Review.* (2019). https://hbr.org/2019/07/6-causes- of-burnout-and-how-to-avoid-them

91 Palmiter, D., Alvord, M., Dorlen, R., Comas-Diaz, L., Luthar, S., Maddi, S., O'Neill, H. K, Saakvitne, K., & Tedeschi, R.G. "Building Your Resilience." *American Psychological Association.* (2012). https://www.apa.org/topics/resilience

92 Sorenson, S., & Garman, K. "How To Tackle U.S. Employees' Stagnating Engagement." *Gallup.* (2013). https://news.gallup.com/

businessjournal/
162953/tackle-employees-stagnating-engagement.aspx

93 Lieberman, C. "What Wellness Programs Don't Do For Workers." *Harvard Business Review*. (2019). https://hbr. org/2019/08/what-wellness-programs-dont-do-for-workers

94 Arora, R., Adhikari, B., & Shetty, D. "Exploring The Relationship Between Employee Engagement And Emotional Intelligence." *Social Science Research Network*. (2015). https://papers.ssrn.com/sol3/papers. cfm?abstract_id=2572514#:~:text=Research%20studies%20have%20 shown%20that,a%20contribution%20of%20emotional%20intelligence.

95 Achor, S., Reece, A., Rosen Kellerman, G., & Robichaux, A. "9 Out Of 10 People Are Willing To Earn Less Money To Do More-Meaningful Work." *Harvard Business Review*. (2018). https://hbr.org/2018/11/9-out-of-10-people-are-willing-to-earn-less-money-to-do-more-meaningful-work

96 Johnson Hess, A. "LinkedIn: 94% Of Employees Say They Would Stay At A Company Longer For This Reason—And It's Not A Raise." *CNBC*. (2019). https://www.cnbc.com/2019/02/27/94percent-of-employees-would-stay-at-a-company-for-this-one-reason.html

97 Baker, M. "Motivate Employees To Reskill For The Digital Age." *Gartner*. (2019). https://www.gartner.com/smarterwithgartner/motivate-employees-to-reskill-for-the-digital-age/

98 O'Donnell, J.T. "Want To Make More Money In 2019? Be Prepared To Prove This 1 Thing To Your Boss." *CNBC*. (2018). https://www.cnbc.com/2018/12/20/to-make-more-money-in-2019-prove-this-1-thing-to-your-boss.html

99 Keng, C. "Employees Who Stay In Companies Longer Than Two Years Get Paid 50% Less." *Forbes*. (2014). https://www.forbes.com/ sites/cameronkeng/2014/06/22/employees-that-stay-in-companies-longer-than-2-years-get-paid-50-less/?sh=121b55a7e07f

100 White, E. "How To Reduce Turnover." *The Wall Street Journal*. (2009). http://guides.wsj.com/management/recruiting-hiring-and-firing/how-to-reduce-employee-turnover/

101 Nolan, T. "The No. 1 Employee Benefit That No One's Talking About." *Gallup*. https://www.gallup.com/

102 Harter, J., & Adkins, A. "What Great Managers Do To Engage Employees." *Harvard Business Review*. (2015). https://hbr. org/2015/04/what-great-managers-do-to-engage-employees

103 Louie, D., Brook, K., & Frates, E. "The Laughter Prescription." *American Journal of Lifestyle Medicine*. (2016). https:// www.ncbi.nlm.nih.gov/pmc/articles/PMC6125057/

104 Suttie, J. "How Laughter Brings Us Together." *Greater Good Magazine.* (2017). https://greatergood.berkeley. edu/article/item/how_laughter_brings_us_together

105 Beheshti, N. "10 Timely Statistics About The Connection Between Employee Engagement And Wellness." *Forbes.* (2010). https://www. forbes.com/sites/nazbeheshti/2019/01/16/10-timely-statistics-about-the-connection-between-employee-engagement-and-wellness/?sh=7792399 022a0

106 "Workplace Well-Being Linked To Senior Leadership Support, New Survey Finds." *American Psychological Association.* (2016). https:// www.apa.org/news/press/releases/2016/06/workplace-well-being

107 Mohn, T. "Take A Vacation: It's Good For Productivity And The Economy, According To A New Study." *Forbes.* (2014). https://www.forbes.com/sites/tanyamohn/2014/02/28/ take-a-vacation-its-good-for-productivity-and-the-economy-according-to-a-new-study/?sh=77e5f01d5a33